Is She
The Doctor's Daughter?

Moira Andrew

Copyright © 2025 Moira Andrew

ISBN: 9798314594995

Published by Publish & Print

All rights reserved. No part of this book may be used or reproduced in any manner whatsoever without written permission from the author

Cover design: Qurat Z (Fiverr.com)
Silver Fish by Philip Tulley

For more information please visit:

www.moiraandrew.com

For Norman, Fiona, Jen, and Mark
And in memory of Allen and Liz

CHAPTER ONE

'He wasn't your real father, you know,' my mother said, crumpling the photograph in restless fingers. A sharp intake of breath, mine. And a moment of complete silence between us.

'Want to sit up a bit?' I asked. I crooked my arm in hers and heaved, building a tower of pillows with the other hand. Her thin once-red hair fanned out. Her rings twirled on bird-bone fingers. She dropped Dad's picture, forgotten, on the bed. She looked tired, dead tired, but she had enough energy left to glare at me from blue malevolent eyes. She knew she had scored a direct hit and intended to enjoy it to the full.

'He's late again,' she said, a half-smile hovering about her lips. 'No idea of time, your dad. Never had.' She pulled herself upright, in charge, as usual, dismissing me. 'I shouldn't wait if I were you.'

I snatched up the photograph before she remembered what she'd done with it and put her used nightie, cardigan and lace-edged handkerchief into a Tesco bag, brought for the purpose. 'Anything else you need, Mum?' I asked. 'Juice? A magazine? Some grapes?' I usually brought her strawberries in sugar, cut-up oranges, something tangy and tempting.

'I wouldn't mind some apples stewed with cloves, you know the way I like them,' she said. I sighed. Seedless grapes would have been a whole lot easier.

'No problem, stewed apples it is,' I said, bending to kiss

the frail cheeks, more bones than flesh these days. 'See you tomorrow.'

No doubt she'd forgotten me by the time I left the ward as she fretted for Dad, worried that he might have met with an accident. 'Drives like a mad thing,' she confided to the nurses every night as she waited in vain for him to arrive, pushing through the swing doors, full of apologies, well-worn leather bag in hand.

*

She hadn't always been this butterfly-brained, I thought. Yes, she could be moody, but the woman my mum used to be was generally pretty organised, if somewhat acerbic.

Remembering the mother of old, unsmiling, severe, ever-ready to take offence, I jostled my way through the brash shopping mall at the entrance. With its coffee shop, Boots the Chemist, its chain store jewellers and bookstall, the reception area was more a downtown street than a hospital nowadays. I emerged through wheezing doors onto a green space where a group of deprived smokers lit up and a cool fountain splashed over stones.

My bus wasn't due for another ten minutes, so I sat on the wall by the fountain and mentally re-ran Mum's outburst. The more I thought about it, the more upset I felt. Dad's death was enough to cope with, but this beat the lot. Had she really said he wasn't my true father? How could she? I'm as like him as peas in a pod, right down to the grey of my eyes and the shape of my nose, I reassured myself. I'm Lucy White, the doctor's daughter

– my Dad's daughter. That's who I am.

*

Thinking back, Mum had always been jealous of our relationship – maybe mothers are always jealous of daughters – and the way he'd put his arm casually around my shoulders, teasing me, a smile lighting up his grey eyes. She hated that he still called me 'Poppet' once I'd reached my teens. 'That girl has a perfectly good name, you know,' she'd say. She hated even more fiercely our shared love of drawing and painting, which she regarded as a waste of time for both of us.

'Put those paints down and do something useful,' she'd hiss in exasperation. 'And don't forget to clear up the mess when you're finished. You can't expect me to tidy up whenever you two choose to dabble. I've more to do with my time – and so, Charles, have you! You can't see patients when you're up to the ears in paint.' And she'd stalk off towards the surgery, head in the air, tut-tutting under her breath.

Dad would arch his eyebrows and shrug, 'Best do what your mother asks PDQ.' Then a glance at his watch, 'No rest for the wicked. Mustn't keep the punters waiting.' And after a quick scrub and a change of clothes, he'd follow my mother through an internal door to his surgery which was attached to the house.

That was the way it used to be before... I tended to think in BDD and ADD terms... Before Dad Died. After Dad Died. And BBC, of course, before the Big C got Mum.

I'd had to grow up a lot – and quickly – since then.

Heavens, I'll miss the bus if I don't get a move on, I thought, almost sprinting to the stop. Nan wouldn't be too pleased if I was late again. 'You've still got homework to do, my girl. You can't expect the world to stop spinning just because your mum's sick, you know.' And it's true. Nan kept my feet on the ground. 'Routine's the best medicine, Lucy-girl,' she told me.

I plumped myself down in an upstairs seat, eye-to-eye with the tops of summer trees. The bus turned the corner into the main road where the shops had gone all Continental with striped sunshades, café tables and chairs on the pavement, flowers gasping for breath in buckets and people in shorts and sun-tops strolling past, too hot to rush.

Then it hit me. Why I hadn't twigged immediately, I'll never know. It made me sweat just to ask the question in the privacy of my head. What on earth did my mother, my prim straight-laced not-much-fun mother think she was doing having a child (me) by a man who wasn't her husband?

Of course, I had no way of knowing what she might have got up to in her fluffier hippier days. It was hard to remember what she was like before she had her personality change. When I was small, she was the kind of mummy you saw in old-fashioned children's picture books, with curly red-gold hair and wide blue eyes. She wore swirling green skirts, and white puff-sleeved blouses, and skipped rather than walked. 'So pretty – like a doll,' Dad's patients said of her. 'Lucky man!'

I knew they'd never say the same of me, the ugly duckling

of the family. But my Dad loved me to bits. Of that, I was absolutely sure – until today. What if the word 'my' was no longer appropriate? How could I bear it?

I scrolled down to Nan's number on my mobile, apologised like mad, lied through my teeth, held up at the hospital, I said, and tumbled off the bus at the next stop. I had to be alone. I had to have time to think.

*

Not that it happened that way. In my blind hurry, I more or less tripped over Henry Davies. 'Hey, watch out,' he said, steadying me. 'Running to catch a bus, are you?'

'No,' I said. 'I've just jumped off the 62.'

'What are you doing here anyway?' Henry pushed his glasses back along his nose. He did this unconsciously all the time. 'I thought you were still with your nan.'

'I am. I simply need some time to think – on my own.'

'I can take a hint,' Henry said.

'It's not that exactly. It's just…'

'About your mum?' Henry guessed.

'Well, it is and it isn't.' But I had to tell someone and I knew that I couldn't face Nan with uncomfortable questions, not at the moment. 'Have you time to listen to a long story?' And it all spilled out. We sat on the wall outside a chiropractor's elegant surgery as cars went streaming past. It was still hot, too hot, in the early evening sunshine. Henry used the bottom of his T-shirt to wipe sweat from his glasses.

Then he said, 'Got any cash on you? I've just enough for one cup of coffee.'

We pooled what we had and went to sit under the green and white sunblind of a smart Italian café. I talked and talked. Henry was a good listener, muttering, 'Mmm,' from time to time and asking the odd question.

I showed him a couple of quick pencil sketches I'd grabbed when she was asleep. In them, she looked thinner than ever and I'd managed to capture the gaunt planes of her face, hair spread out over the pillow, but they weren't exactly flattering.

'Is she really as thin as this?' Henry asked. 'And her hair, it's like a fountain – I seem to remember it all twisted up into some kind of bun-like thing.'

Astute, I thought, but that's what I like about Henry. He notices things. He's one of those people who seems to have been around all my life. Older than me, serious, a bit of a brain, off-hand sometimes. 'But reliable,' I had assured my Dad when we went off on bikes, Henry to look for fossils, me with my ever-present sketchbook.

'Reliable?' Dad had laughed. 'Sounds more like a used car than a boyfriend.'

'Henry is not boyfriend material,' I told him. 'He's more of a mate, just a friend really.' The idea of snogging with the sombre Henry, let alone anything sexier, was out of the question. Nan understood. 'He was born middle-aged, that young man,' she said.

But he was just what the doctor ordered this summer evening. 'Don't jump to conclusions,' he advised me. 'Take your time. See if you can find old letters, photographs, your birth certificate – anything at all.'

'Good idea,' I said, 'but I don't seem to have a spare minute these days.' I looked at my watch and shoved the sketchbook to the bottom of my bag. 'Must go. Nan will be having conniptions by now. Thanks, Henry.'

'No problem. I'll work on it,' Henry promised. He pulled a paperback from his pocket and was instantly lost in it. 'See you around.' He flapped his hand at me in a desultory way, left coins in the saucer and was off up the road, head in a book. I waited at the bus stop, feeling less ripped apart than before.

I was out of breath and out of sorts by the time I arrived at Nan's little terraced house on the other side of town. 'Where have you been?' she greeted me but didn't wait for an answer. That was Nan all over. I was home and safe. Time to move on.

I spread my homework on the table and sat by the open window, looking out onto Nan's yard. Nothing special, yet it brimmed with colour – geraniums, petunias, begonias and fuchsias all higgledy-piggledy in tubs and pots among ivies and other green plants that I couldn't begin to identify. My fingers ached to get the scene down on paper, but there wasn't time. Time was short for most things in life these days.

Nan was out in the yard, hose in hand, in her element. 'Finished?' she called. 'Come and join me when you're done.

It's lovely and cool outside.'

'Nan,' I said, 'have we any apples left? Mum would like some stewed with cloves for tomorrow.'

'Anything else Madam wants?' Nan could be quite caustic about Mum, cancer or no cancer. 'You'll need to pop down to the Spar and get some. If you get a move on, you'll just make it.'

I grabbed some money from the housekeeping tin and went from Nan's front door straight into the street. She was right. It was cool and just beginning to turn a purply dark, like a faded bruise.

I thought about how much Dad would have enjoyed catching the scene in acrylic, scribbling tree shapes against the deepening sky, using his thumb to suggest the summer-heavy leaves, finding a mix of greys and blues for the terraced houses, pinpointing the odd white flower with a dab of his brush. He had been a wonderful GP general practitioner and his patients had loved him, but if things had turned out differently, he could have been a highly successful professional artist – in my opinion at least. Once he'd had some paintings exhibited in a small out-of-town gallery, but none had sold. 'Back to the day job,' he'd joked, as he stacked the canvases back in the loft. Despite his deprecating laughter, I reckon his pride was deeply hurt.

*

Swinging the apples in a plastic bag, I sauntered home – well, to Nan's – not home to the house where Dad and Mum and I had lived BDD. I tried to push the memory of that terrible night to the back of my brain, but in spite of my efforts, it sometimes ran round and round in a loop. Five days to Christmas, me in front of the television, Mum with one of her headaches, the telephone shrilling.

'Do me a favour, Lucy, please answer that wretched thing.' I did, but the line went dead immediately. I heard the receiver being put down. It was a gentle sound, not a slam. We'd had a lots of calls like this recently.

Mum and I were used to being alone in the house. More often than not, especially lately, Dad had been out on a late call. 'That's what being a GP is all about,' he'd say. 'Being there when you're needed.' I felt very proud of him.

Then the doorbell rang.

'What now?' Mum said. 'Can you get it, Lucy? Make sure the chain's on the door.' That's the trouble with having a surgery in the house. People call at all hours.

Two police constables, a man and a woman, shuffled about on the step, their breath making dragon smoke in the winter air. They showed me their ID. 'Is Mrs White at home?' they asked.

'Can't I take a message?' I was used to out-of-hours calls.

'It's very urgent. I must talk to Mrs White – your mother?' I nodded. They asked to come inside.

'Mum, it's for you!' I called and the nightmare began in earnest. A stray dog, a slick of ice, a brick wall. 'Nothing anyone could do. I'm so sorry. Is there someone with you? A friend we can call?'

Mum, voice icily controlled, face masked in her polite mode, thanked the officers. 'My daughter and I would like to be alone. I'm sure you understand,' she said firmly. She ushered them out and they went reluctantly towards their car. Officialdom could wait. Dad was dead.

'I just knew he'd do something stupid one of these days,' Mum muttered to herself when they'd gone. 'Drives like a mad thing.' She perched on the edge of a chair, hugging her knees. She didn't cry. 'I keep telling him, but he won't listen. Stupid, stupid, stupid...' she repeated over and over.

I don't think she was aware of me, didn't even notice that I was in the same room, until the choked-up tears began to roll down my cheeks. 'Dad... 'I whimpered, 'Dad...'

My lovely dad – inside my head, I could see his face with smiley grey eyes, feel the gentle fingers ruffle my hair, hear the deep rumbling laugh that started at the bottom of his throat. But never again, not for real. 'No! Please no!' I pleaded aloud.

'Stop it!' Mum snapped. 'Crying won't bring him back. It's time you went to bed, Lucy. I'd have a hot bath if I were you,' she suggested. Just as if it were an ordinary night.

I didn't know what to do. 'Cup of tea? Glass of wine?' I asked. But she didn't answer, simply sat there rocking and muttering to herself. She was completely out of it, I realised.

'Should we phone Nan?'

'Nan! Not Nan, of all people. 'Where's your imagination, girl. Really!' I left her alone and crawled upstairs to bed.

Hate for the unknown patient welled up inside me. If only he hadn't been called out. If only the dog hadn't been on the loose, the road iced up. If only… I cried myself to sleep.

CHAPTER TWO

Mum was never the same after Dad's accident. Sometimes she lost it and took to gazing out of the window waiting for him to come back. 'He's late again tonight,' she'd complain. 'Patients have no consideration. They think doctors have no beds to go to.'

At other times, she was all go, signing papers, writing cheques, making lists, and answering calls. 'Your mother's so brave,' neighbours said. 'She's coping magnificently.'

But she wasn't, of course. And I was the only person who knew what was really happening – that she hardly ate a thing, just cups of weak tea and an occasional slice of toast. She grew as thin as a twig and her lovely hair began to lose its lustre. I worried about her a lot, but she wouldn't listen to me. 'You know nothing,' she'd say. 'You're just a child, remember.'

Everything I said or did was wrong. 'Doctor?' she'd say. 'I don't need a doctor. I'm married to one.'

'But Dad's dead.'

'Who says?'

I spoke to Nan on the quiet, but Mum wouldn't hear of her coming to see us. 'Bad enough she had to be at the funeral, without inviting her here.'

'But Mum…'

'Don't but Mum me – we're OK Lucy. We're a team.'

That was news to me. However, I'd go over to her, put my arm round her shoulders. She pulled away from anything more intimate. She hadn't been a kissing mum for a long time. I had a vague memory of playing with her long hair when I was little, unrolling a red-gold curl with my finger and watching it twist back like a spring. No chance of that game now. For years she'd worn it pinned-up, scraped back behind her ears. She wore an invisible DON'T TOUCH label around her neck.

'Mum, remember the accident – you know Dad's dead, don't you?'

'No, he's not. He's just late. Honestly, the ideas you get into your head sometimes! I can't keep up with you. Too many books, too much television.' And she'd go back to rocking in her chair.

After the funeral and the first flush of visitors, nobody disturbed us much. Mum put everyone off. When they called, she'd say, 'Lucy, tell them not this afternoon. Tell them I'm busy.' Gradually, the calls stopped coming. Nan was firmly warned off, although I secretly kept in touch.

*

I had always known about Mum's cruel streak, but she gave it full rein after Dad's death – when she accepted it, that is. True, she had lost her husband, but he was my father and Nan's son as well. This fact was conveniently shelved to the back of her mind. Our grief wasn't in the same street as hers.

Nan took refuge in stoic silence, saying only, 'Everyone has their own way of dealing with things,' and kept her distance. If pushed, she'd add, 'Grace was always a bit odd.'

When Dad's accountant, the vicar and the man from the British Medical Association arrived, Mum rallied and talked quite rationally, as far as I could make out. For weeks, the car sat immobile in the drive. She gave me her PIN so that I could take money from the hole in the wall, and I got most of the things we needed from the corner shop.

And that's how we managed through the long winter months. The internal door to the surgery was bricked up and a locum took over the practice. All the surgery calls were transferred to another line. The house was spookily quiet.

Most nights I dreamed about dad. 'Daddy,' I'd hear myself say. 'Can I have a ride on your shoulders? Daddy, can I come in the car with you?' Or more often, 'Daddy, can I go drawing with you?' I was always a small child in my dreams. But I was never able to touch him. He was always just out of reach. I'd wake up disappointed, so near yet so far, his death new each morning.

Mum was either wrapped up in her own grief, cold and even more unapproachable than usual, or angry, when she had forgotten about the accident and was waiting for his return. Her mind was like a jumping flea.

It was term-time, so I went to school as though nothing had happened, made my sandwiches, did my homework and hoped like mad that things would get better. I didn't have time for friends. Even Millie got frozen out and stopped calling.

Some days Mum took to staying in bed for most of the

morning. When she finally got up she'd sit by the gas fire, not reading, not watching television, just sitting, muttering under her breath. Sometimes she went on grand cleaning sprees, emptying drawers and filling charity bags, never at ease with herself.

'It's somewhere here, I know it is… but where?' The living room looked as though it had been burgled, stuff scattered all over the floor.

'What are you looking for? Can I help?' I'd ask.

'No, Lucy, you wouldn't understand. I'll get my hands on it if it's the last thing I do.' And she was off again, raking through our possessions like a rag-and-bone man. I even caught her tearing up a photograph of me as a toddler, sitting high on Dad's shoulders, sunhat on askew, squinting into the sun.

'Please Mum, may I have it?'

Reluctantly she passed the pieces over to me. 'On your own head be it,' she said. She often said funny things these days.

She'd tire herself out. Then she was off again. 'He's hidden it. I know he has. Thinks he'll get away with it, but I'll show him.'

'Dad?' I ventured.

'Who else? Brings it on himself, you know. Secrecy is a terrible trait in a married man.' What was she on about? My father was the most open character in the world. 'I'll have words with him when he comes back – if he ever does.' No use reminding her when she was in one of those moods. It was truly scary.

'I've ordered a skip,' she said one day. 'I'm clearing

every last piece of junk out of this house. It depresses me, seeing your Dad's stuff lying around. He's dead, you know.' Was reality sinking in at last? 'When I feel a bit better, you can help me clear the attic?'

'But Dad's paintings are up there,' I protested.

'Exactly,' Mum said. 'I intend to get shot of the lot. It's the only answer.' I prayed that she wouldn't have the stamina to pull down the loft ladder by herself and always found a ready excuse when she enlisted my help.

It came to a head one Saturday afternoon. I was in the garden scribbling down some storyboard ideas for a Shakespeare project I was doing with Millie – the pictures were my contribution, the words hers. I heard a strange rumbling noise from upstairs, a scream, an ominous silence. Everything became a blur. Mum had tripped and fallen from the loft ladder. She lay in an untidy heap on the landing. 'It's bad luck. Get rid of it,' she gasped. I didn't know what she was on about, but I'd have said 'yes' to anything.

An ambulance, Mum as floppy as a puppet with broken strings, telephone calls, blue lights, doctors looking grim. Not because of the fall – as it turned out, she was only bruised – not grief, not depression, but the Big C itself. It had been eating her from the inside out.

'She did herself a favour in a way,' they said at the hospital. 'We may have caught it in time – if luck's on our side.' Nan and I knew what they meant by 'it,' cancer, the Big C.

I reached the corner of Nan's road, convinced that I could hear footsteps behind me. I stopped. The footsteps stopped. I looked round. In the dim light, I saw a girl about my own age.

'Excuse me,' she said. 'Are you Doctor White's daughter?'

'Why do you want to know?' Well, you can't be too careful about talking to strangers, even teenage girls, at ten o'clock at night.

'Just wondered. I heard you were staying around here somewhere, with your granny are you?'

'As it happens, I am. So? What's it got to do with you?' I'd had a hard day and didn't feel sociable. The girl fell into step beside me. She peered at me in the last of the shadowy light.

'You look just like him, you know. It's uncanny,' she said.

'Are you one of my father's patients?' I asked, curiosity getting the better of me.

'Yes and no,' she said. 'Mostly it was my mother he came to see. Of course, I saw him too when he came to our house. And we saw a lot of him lately.' She stopped suddenly. 'I live up this way. Bye. See you again, no doubt.' And she vanished, almost melting into the park railings at the corner of the street.

Strange, I thought, putting the encounter to the back of my mind. I was more interested in seeing if I could persuade Nan to do Mum's apples for me. I was hot and tired and in no mood to peel apples, let alone find a jar of cloves for the finishing touch.

17

But I needn't have worried.

'Give these here,' Nan said as soon as I got in. 'And off to bed with you. You have a maths test tomorrow, didn't you say?'

She was wonderful, my Nan. Imagine remembering the wretched maths test. More than Mum would have done, even when she was well. 'Thanks, Nan,' I said and kissed her.

She flipped me gently with a tea towel. 'No need to fuss,' she said. But you could see from her eyes that she had a soft spot for me.

I lay outside the duvet, window open, curtains wide. The summer air was so thick, that you could have stirred the left-over heat with a spoon. Amplified voices rose from the hugger-mugger walled yards and open doors. Not a night for sleep, especially when I thought about what Mum had said. And the way she had looked at me. With malice, I thought. Not a nice thing to have to say about your own mother.

I plugged my CD player into my ears, moronic stuff, but I didn't care. Drifting off, it came to me – maybe I'm adopted? No, it couldn't be that. She was always reminding me what a hard time I'd given her. 'Thirty-six hours of pure agony. What we women have to put up with!' she'd say every time my birthday came around.

My brain was wound up. I couldn't stop thinking. If my dad wasn't my Dad, where had I come from? Perhaps I'm a donor baby, what did they call it? AID, sounds a lot like Aids, but it means something different, artificial insemination by donor, I think. Sounds disgusting. I don't reckon my Mum would be up for it.

A lover, then. I know that Mum and Dad went about in a crowd when he was at university, girlfriends, boyfriends, best mates, that kind of thing. I remembered a photograph of them posing on an old banger, his first car, hanging out of the windows, sitting on the bonnet.

Mum looked different from the others, even then. She was kind of hippy with her halo of hair and long coloured skirts. Not for her the jeans and top uniform everyone else wore, hair raked back into a ponytail. What had Dad seen in her? Was it the long rippling hair, or just that she didn't conform?

And hot on its heels, another question. Was one of these blokes my real father? Impossible. Dad is my dad – and that's it.

*

The math test was every bit as ghastly as I thought it would be. 'Can't hang around,' I told Millie, who was standing by the door with the others picking over the test, 'Got to get to the hospital.' Conversation stopper.

'Sorry, I forgot… Poor you… How is your Mum?' floated after me. I thought fleetingly about how much I missed Millie, Sheenagh and the gang, but I had no time to dwell on it. I had to scarper to pick up Mum's clean stuff, a magazine and the apples Nan had left in a jar in the fridge. Nan was still at work, in the old people's home. Maybe that's why she didn't have much time for

Mum's fads and fancies.

I grabbed a chocolate biscuit and made it to the stop just as the bus arrived. Out of breath, I heaved myself and my carrier bag into a seat by the window.

'Mind if I join you?' a voice asked. 'You *are* Dr White's daughter, aren't you?'

'Didn't I see you last night? Outside the Spar?'

I could have a better look at her this time. She was blonde, quite plump, grey-eyed. 'Might have done,' she said.

'Oh, come on. You told me that my dad was your mum's doctor, didn't you?'

'Might have done. Must go. See you around.' Then she turned back, 'You a friend of Henry Davies?' she asked.

'What's it to do with you? Who are you anyway?' I had reached the end of my patience.

'My name's Mariella. Ask your mum or your grandma about me. Or Henry, next time you bump into him.' At that, she ran downstairs and leapt off the bus. Quite a nifty jump for a girl her size, I thought. Miaow.

*

Mum looked more faded than ever. 'We're a bit worried,' the nurse said. 'She's not responding to the new treatment as she should. Try not to upset her.' And she soft-shoe shuffled out into the corridor.

But I never upset her. Well, not knowingly, I said to myself, as I bent to kiss the fragile cheek. 'I brought you apples,'

I said. 'Stewed with cloves, the way you like them.'

'Thanks, love,' she whispered. At least she seemed to know who I was. 'Seen Dad today?'

'About dad...' I started, but I had no idea how to go on. I'd tried every trick in the book. So, I plunged into a different topic. 'Mum, does the name Mariella mean anything to you?'

'Mariella? *Mariella?* Mum almost spat out the name. Then she tried to sit up, bright spots appearing on her pale cheeks. 'You haven't brought her here, have you?' She was really wound up. Then she went back to her old game of blackmail. 'Lucy, you're bringing on one of my heads. Go away, if that's the best you can do.'

'But, Mum. I've just come. I've brought you a copy of this month's *Two's Company*. And your clean stuff.'

At that she perked up a bit, suddenly appearing to forget all about the Mariella thing and I certainly had no intention of returning to it. Then an unexpected flash of motherly concern.

'Is Nan looking after you? Why she doesn't come to see me, I can't think. True, I'm not her flesh and blood, but I'm the next best thing.'

'You told her not to, Mum. Remember?'

'Did I?' she asked, sounding bewildered.

How could she have forgotten the scene? It had been utterly cringe-making. Mum had screamed at Nan, 'Happy now, you ole witch? Never good enough for your precious son, was I?' And lots more in the same vein. Then, 'Get out and don't come back. Ever.'

The staff tried to put a gloss on the outburst. 'Take no notice,' they said. 'She doesn't know what she's saying.'

'She does, you know,' Nan said quietly. 'She's been waiting a long time to have a go at me. I'll be down in the concourse when you're ready, Lucy.' Then she walked away with perfect dignity.

Now Mum fretted, murmuring, 'Where's that Dad of yours?' He hasn't turned up for days. I don't know what's the matter with him. You'd think a doctor, of all people, wouldn't be frightened of visiting a hospital.'

The sister put her head round the door. 'Your mum's tired out, poor dear,' she said. Mum would hate the 'poor dear' bit, I thought. I hope she's not listening. I put her things away, kissed her and followed the sister out.

'Is it the drugs?' I asked. 'She seems to come and go.'

'Well, they can have that effect. At least she's not in pain. But we think there must be more to it than that – she's quite lucid at times, then off she goes into a world of her own.' The sister produced a sheaf of notes. 'Is she usually this disorientated?'

I didn't know what to say. I didn't want to let Mum down. 'Occasionally... not often,' I said, knowing that was a mega-lie.

'Is there anyone else we can contact? Sisters? Brothers?' I shook my head. 'There's a Katherine White, your grandmother, yes?'

I nodded. 'But they don't get on. Mum would have a fit if

she arrived out of the blue. There's nobody else. Mum's a pretty private kind of person.'

'She keeps asking for your father, but she's a widow, isn't she?'

'Yes, Dad's dead,' I said, tears filling my eyes. It happens that way sometimes, when I have to say the word 'dead' out loud. I rushed down the corridor as fast as my legs would take me. When I managed to make it to the outside world, I found not only that strange girl, Mariella waiting for me, but Henry too. He was standing behind her, looking distinctly sheepish.

'What's this?' I asked. 'A reception committee?'

'Odd question. Have you time to come back to Mariella's house?' Henry, shifting uneasily from one foot to the other, would rather have been somewhere, anywhere else, I could tell.

'It's near Nan's, isn't it? I'll see what she says.' This was playing for time. I didn't usually discuss my comings and goings with Nan and she didn't expect it. She trusted me.

'Don't tell your grandma where I live, please don't,' Mariella said. She sounded really anxious. 'It won't take long, I promise.' So, despite my better judgement, I agreed. After all, Henry would be there too.

But it turned out Henry had no intention of coming along. He had simply engineered the meeting. Then he sloped off, saying he'd text me. Text me? Henry? That idea was nearly as surprising as being whisked off to a secret mission at Mariella's.

We bussed it down to the old town. 'Along here,' Mariella

said and I followed her along a street of terraced houses, much like Nan's place, but a lot more ramshackle.

It was the last house in the street, where we went down some steps into a basement. 'A garden flat, if you're feeling kind,' Mariella said, as she took a key from her pocket and fiddled around in the keyhole. She gave the door a mighty push and more or less fell into the hallway.

Despite the sunshine, the flat was dark and shadowy, like going into a *Borrower's* hole. Mariella took me into the kitchen which smelt fusty, of old best-forgotten meals.

'Like a coffee?' she asked. 'I think I've – we've – still got some milk left.' I don't know a lot about refrigerators, but this one looked grim.

'No thanks, I had one at the hospital,' I lied.

'Wait a minute,' Mariella said. 'I've got something to show you.' I heard her rummaging around in the next room. She came back with a picture, blowing dust off the glass. 'Recognise it?' she asked.

CHAPTER THREE

Recognise it? I'd have known his stuff at twenty paces.

'My Dad painted that,' I said. It was done in dad's trademark layered acrylic, just blobs of colour close-up, but a rocky sea scene with gulls and a couple of orange sailing boats if you stood far enough back. I couldn't quite identify the place, but it felt vaguely familiar and I had the oddest feeling that I'd once been there. Weird, I thought. I turned the picture over, but there were no clues on the back. This not-knowing was going to niggle at me.

'Any idea where this place is?' I asked.

'Nope. West Wales, somewhere, at a guess.' Mariella shrugged. 'It belongs to my mother – and I know that she likes it a lot. I just wanted to check with you that it's a genuine Charles White.' She seemed pretty jumpy and didn't quite know what to say next. 'Thanks for coming,' she finally managed.

I found myself being propelled towards the door. 'Don't tell anyone you've been here, please. Please...' she begged. 'They'd take me away if they knew.'

'You mean you're here on your own? Just you?' She nodded. 'And nobody knows?'

'Well, Henry does,' she admitted. 'And now you, of course. But please don't say anything. Not till I get things sorted out.'

I was reluctant, but Mariella looked distinctly scared.

'Okay,' I said. 'Not a word.' For the first time, she smiled. Quite pretty, I thought, when she smiles. I wonder if Henry fancies her? More to old Henry than meets the eye, I thought.

'You're a pal,' Mariella said. Then, 'I didn't expect to like you, but you're all right.'

What on earth had I done to her? I wondered. After all, I'd only just met her. I shrugged it off. I had more pressing things to worry about.

*

I walked back towards Nan's. Perhaps she'd be able to put me in the picture about this odd girl. I'd promised not to give her secret away, so I'd have to be pretty careful about what I said.

Nan wasn't home. I mooched around the empty house, positively aching for my dad. He'd have known how to cope – with mum and her cancer, with me and my skittering thoughts. For sure, he'd have laughed off Mum's wacky ideas and set my mind at rest.

I poured myself a cold drink, opened the back door to the still-sweltering heat and flopped down on Nan's ancient couch.

I couldn't get Mariella's picture out of my head. It came and went like a video on the blink. The more I thought about it, the more familiar it seemed. I was sure as eggs that once, long ago, I'd walked along that bit of shore. I struggled to picture it. In the back of my brain, I had a dim sense of being in a cave among the rocks. I remember hearing the hush of the waves, being shut in, and feeling frightened.

Where on earth was it? How did one of Dad's paintings come to be hanging on this strange girl's wall? And who the hell was Mariella anyway?

If I'd had the energy, I'd have doodled my half-remembered version of the scene in the picture, but I simply couldn't be bothered. It all seemed too much like hard work today, although I knew perfectly well that getting my drawing things out would help settle my thoughts. Later perhaps, once it grew cooler.

My mobile trembled. A text from Henry. This was a first! *HI Lus, Sry abt 2day. Mst spk 2 U urgent. Luv H.* Well, he said 'love.' That was another first. But it explained nothing.

*

Nan exploded into the house. 'Lucy?' she called. 'Any hope of a coffee?' She threw herself down beside me. 'I must have walked a hundred miles today. It was 'Kath this' and 'Kath that,' poor things, feeling the heat just like the rest of us. My feet are killing me.' She kicked off her sandals.

I made her a coffee, hot and strong, just the way she likes it. 'Thanks love,' she said. 'And how was your day?'

Where to start? 'Mum's not too good,' I ventured. 'She's away with the bees half the time, still refusing to accept that Dad's dead. Then completely with it in the next breath.'

'That's nothing new,' Nan said. 'She's always been a bit strange, that one. She used to skip down the road in a green nightgown – in the middle of the afternoon, if you please –

chanting some outlandish gibberish, as often as not. She was the talk of the neighbourhood at one time. But your dad would never have a word said against her, no matter what.'

It didn't sound like the laced-up mother I knew, but there are some things that children never hear about.

'She could twist your dad round her little finger, easy as pie. She couldn't stand it when you started to cry, you know. "Get that baby out of here!" she'd shout – she never did understand that babies and dollies were two different things.' Nan sipped her coffee. 'To keep the peace your dad used to bring you round to me. Anything for a quiet life, that was my Charles all over.'

I knew that I'd never been the apple of my mother's eye, but I didn't think it was this bad. Nan went silent, remembering and, for a moment, I thought she might cry. Was this the time to bring Mariella into the conversation? I wouldn't say where she lived, of course. I got myself psyched up.

'Nan?' I began, but at that minute another text announced itself, also from Henry. So I changed mid-question to, 'Okay if I see Henry for a bit? You put your feet up and I'll be back in time for tea.'

Inspiration! I remembered seeing a half-bottle of white wine in the fridge, so I poured Nan a glass, put the TV remote in her hand and scampered outside.

*

Henry was propped up against the wall. 'What's the panic?' I asked.

'I've been thinking,' he said. 'You know that business about your dad – what your mum said. Well, I don't know about that exactly, but I've discovered – sort of – whose father he *is*.'

'Go on, surprise me.'

'You're not going to like this. I'm almost sure that your dad is Mariella's dad too.' Henry's eyes widened behind his glasses, excitement over his discovery or concern for me. I couldn't make out which.

'You mean that spooky creature's my sister? Pull the other one, it's got bells on,' I said. Plump, blonde, grey-eyed, Mariella isn't the least like me, I thought – well, maybe the eyes, but hundreds of people have grey eyes. 'What gives you that idea?'

'I don't know the full story,' Henry said. 'But I do know that your dad was a frequent visitor to Mariella's place – and that he was with her mother the night he died.'

'So? She was Dad's patient.'

'And he had Christmas presents for both of them. Not the typical behaviour of your average local doctor, I guess.' Henry was doing his earnest best. 'If you don't – won't – believe me, ask your Nan. She knows all about it.'

'What's this sudden interest in this Mariella person anyway?' I had to ask. Henry and I had been friends, if not exactly an item, for years and I felt a distinct stab of jealousy.

'Oh, we're two of a kind, Mariella and me, trying to make the best of things on our own. You're lucky, you know, with your

Nan around.' I knew, of course in a vague kind of way that Henry was living alone in some kind of bed-sit. He considered for a moment, obviously weighing his next words. 'Her mother's disappeared, I forgot to tell you that. She came to your Dad's funeral, of course, but afterwards, she couldn't cope, so she upped sticks and left.'

'Mariella's mother came to my Dad's funeral?' I was so angry, red-mist-down-over-the-eyes angry, that I simply didn't care about anyone else in the world, neither Mariella nor her mother. 'Well, thank you very much, Henry Davies. That's just what I needed to know.'

What do they say about blaming the messenger? I stalked off, furious at Henry. 'I'll see you sometime, I expect.' I didn't want him to see the jealous tears I was attempting to scrub away. With a tear-stained face and hair stuck to my scalp with sweat, I was not a pretty sight, not by any stretch of the imagination.

'Luce, I'm sorry,' Henry said, coming after me. He turned my face towards his. My God, I thought, he's going to kiss me. But no, not Henry. He touched my cheek. 'Remember, I'm here if you need me.' He loped off down the road and didn't look back.

Despite the heat, I legged it back to Nan's. There was nothing else for it. I had to find out right now what she knew about the dreaded Mariella.

*

Nan had ordered a pizza for supper. She had opened the doors and windows, but still the hot air sloshed around the room. It was difficult to breathe. 'Nan?' I said. 'Does the name Mariella mean anything to you?'

'I wondered when you'd find out,' Nan said. 'I used to say they should tell you who she is, but they wouldn't have it, neither of them.'

'Who is she?'

Nan took a deep breath. 'Mariella is your half-sister – your dad's love child, to put it bluntly.'

'Love-child?' So, Henry was right. 'But Dad loved me,' I said in a small voice.

'Of course he did,' Nan reassured me. 'That's just an old-fashioned way of saying that Mariella's mother and your dad were… had a relationship.'

What they call 'a bit on the side,' I thought. So where does that leave me?

The doorbell rang and we had the business of dividing up the pizza, finding plates, and pouring drinks. I didn't think I was hungry, but I ate up every scrap. We put the dishes in the sink and sat outside in the relative cool of the yard.

'So how did it happen, Nan?' I asked.

'I don't know the whole story, of course, but I'll tell you as much as I can.' I shivered. 'Cold?' Nan asked.

'No,' I said. 'Just a ghost walking over my grave.' Nan drew her chair closer to mine.

'When your dad, my Charles, went to medical school, he got into a real rowdy crowd. Maybe he needed to, especially when he got to the blood and guts and cutting-up bit of his training. He always was a bit of a tender flower, come to think.' Nan smiled, picturing him.

'Nan, Mariella...' I reminded her.

'Have patience,' Nan said. 'Medicine wasn't the job for your dad - he only did it to please your granddad, you know. He should have been an artist.'

'He was an artist,' I objected.

'No,' said Nan. 'He was a GP who painted. But his heart wasn't in doctoring. Even as a student, he took time off to go to a life class – you know what a life class is?'

'Yes, the nude bit.'

'That's where he met your mother.'

'You mean, she tried painting too?' I couldn't fit Mum into the amateur artist box. As far as I knew, she was totally against anything to do with paints and brushes.

'No,' said Nan. 'She was the model.'

I spluttered with disbelief, but Nan ploughed on. 'There was always a great mystery about your mother, no family, no money, so she said. I suppose she did modelling to earn some cash.'

Thinking back, Mum had always been extremely touchy about her side of the family. 'But do I have another Grandma? A Grandad?' I used to ask.

'Ask no questions, tell no lies,' Mum would say, putting a finger to her lips and moving on to a different topic – washing-up, homework, shopping. Anything to avoid talking about where she came from.

I knew all about Nan, of course and could just remember Grandpa White who smelt of pipe smoke and peppermints. He had sold herbal remedies and medicines and his leather boxes filled with mysterious little blue bottles were still locked away in a cupboard in Nan's front room. It was he who had encouraged Dad to become a doctor, something he'd dearly wanted for himself.

'I couldn't have disappointed Grandpa, it meant so much to him, so art school had to go and medicine it was,' Dad had told me once, sort of sighing and coughing at the same time – putting a brave face on it, I expect. 'I'm a lucky man,' he'd continued, 'two beautiful women in my family and a wonderful mother and father. Not like your poor Mum. She never knew her parents.'

'She was an orphan, you mean?'

'Well, yes in a way.' He didn't sound any too sure himself. 'She won't talk about it much, even to me. But she's had a tough time of it, so try not to nag her, there's a good girl.' So, Mum's family was a no-go area. She was just Mum, once Grace Williams, now Grace White, no middle name, no history. And somehow everybody accepted it, even Nan.

*

'Your mother was always a good-looking woman, in a fragile kind of way,' she said now. 'Painfully thin, but your dad fell for her hook line and sinker. She was like a magnet to a man, petite and perfect.' So that's how my dad was bowled over!

'I didn't take to her much – and I think she knew it. Not like your father who couldn't get enough of her. He wanted nothing more than to be able to draw and paint her day and night, clothed or naked, it didn't matter, even if he had to marry her first. He must have produced dozens of portraits,' Nan mused. 'He used to rave about her translucent skin, *born in the rain,* he once said.'

'Born in the rain,' - that's my dad, I thought. He was always a romantic. But it gave a new perspective on the buttoned-up mother I'd lived with all these years. 'Any idea where the portraits are?' I asked. Dad had always stuck to landscapes as far as I was aware.

'I don't think he was ever allowed to paint her again after they were married. I reckon your mother was ashamed of being a model. I gather she got rid of every last picture – she hated the nude ones most of all. She tore them up in a fit of rage and threw them into the AGA - your dad admitted as much to me when things got rough between them.'

A cool breeze took the edge off the heat. Nan poked her fingers into the nearest flower pot. 'Dry as a bone,' she sighed. 'They'll need a drink before bedtime.'

'I'll give you a hand,' I said. We worked quietly together to the splash of the hose and the drizzle of a watering can, my unexpected half-sister all but forgotten. I had even more on my mind now. The geraniums glowed redder, the penstemons pinker as the summer night turned grey. 'Finished,' we said, almost as one voice, and went inside.

We left the curtains open and, as bats cartwheeled in the yard, Nan talked. I think it was easier for her in the dark. 'Your mother was never a well woman, nice enough, I suppose, but she had a fey way with her, *'tickled by witches'* your dad used to say. With that gorgeous red-gold hair, slim figure – she'd no more than a couple of buttons for breasts – and long elegant legs, she seemed only half-human. All the men were after her, but she had eyes only for your dad, the doctor.'

I knew that Mum had loved Dad to distraction, although she had a peculiar way of showing it. She was jealous of everyone else in his life, from his University friends, through Nan to me.

'It took her years to learn to behave like a proper grown-up person, you know. I remember she liked to play what she called 'mummies and daddies' among the dunes by the sea. It caused a bit of a scandal!' Nan went on.

My eyes widened at this idea. 'No, it's not what you think, Lucy-girl. Your mum had no normal teenage interest in sex, none at all, if your dad was to be believed. All she wanted was to play at houses and be Dr. and Mrs. White without the going-to-bed bit. She even took little cups and saucers and things and laid out elaborate pretend tea parties on the sand.'

'How on earth did Dad fall for this?' I asked, as a faint memory began to take shape in my mind.

'Truth to tell,' Nan said, 'I think he was bewitched.'

That figured, I thought, remembering how Dad always

seemed to be on the receiving end of Mum's temper, but ever-ready to back down and let her have her way.

'Your mother needed security. I think she felt let down. I mean, he never got to be a consultant, never even made money from his paintings. In short, he was neither rich enough, nor famous enough for her.'

'And he found someone else?'

'He did,' Nan said. 'He met Mariella's mother. That was when the balloon went up.'

A funny way of putting it, I thought. But I'd had enough information for one night. 'Nan,' I said, 'I'm tired. I think I'll go up to bed.'

I gave her a quick kiss. Compared to Mum's paper-thin skin, Nan has a proper cuddly face, she's so much more solid than Mum, I thought - in every way.

I lay in bed, my head too full of unanswered questions to let me sleep. The tea party on the sand had triggered off an idea. I brought out all my rags of memory and hung them on the line.

CHAPTER FOUR

'Tea, darling? With milk and two lumps?' I could hear the bell-like voice. 'That's a good girl. Now wipe your hands,' it went on. I'm nearly positive that the cups were empty. We were just playing, pretending. 'Having such fun, aren't we, darling?'

I could hear the waves lapping the shore, gulls screaming in the sky, the breeze whispering in the dunes, but no children's voices. We were alone, my mother and I – and where was Dad?

I remember how the sea lured the small child I was to splash in the shallows, how I longed to feel the cool wetness of the waves between my bare toes. 'Can I paddle, please Mummy?' I pleaded, I cried, to no avail.

'Certainly not!' The voice had lost its sweetness. 'You'll get your beautiful dress dirty.' But I was a determined child. I ran on down to the shore.

'Lucy, you're a bad girl. Come back, come back at once!' When she had disentangled herself from her long skirts, she was after me. My mother's voice sounded shrill and angry. 'Come back here, this minute!' So, I opened my mouth and yelled in frustration like any other small girl.

That did it. She yanked me away from the water by the wrist. I can still remember how painful that was, as my mother half-carried me, and half-dragged me over the rocks. She pushed me roughly into a cave. Out of the sun, it was suddenly cold. There was nothing but echoing emptiness. I was too frightened to cry and simply curled myself into a ball and waited.

I don't know how long I was left there, huddling against the dank rocks, listening to the hush of the waves below. At last, I heard my Dad come back, 'How are my two beautiful girls getting on? Have you finished your picnic? Left something for me, I hope?' Mum must have been packing things away.

Then, 'Where's Lucy? You didn't let her go down to the sea on her own? Grace, you promised... Lucy! Lucy! Lucy!' He was shouting now, panic in his voice.

At last, I was enveloped in a bear hug, loving the feel of his bristly chin, the sharp smell of paint on his fingers. He held me high and safe, smothering me with kisses, crumpling the now sand-soiled frilly dress. As we made for the car, my mother complained, 'Look at the mess she's made of her dress, Charles. It will never be the same again. And we were having such fun, weren't we darling?'

'Damn silly get-up for a child to wear on the beach,' he muttered. Come to think of it, Mum's long flouncy green dress wasn't entirely suited to a picnic on the sand either. It would have looked more at home at a formal party. But Dad knew better than to comment.

'Never mind, Poppet, we'll be home soon,' he said, settling me in my car seat. 'A hot bath and a story and you'll be as right as rain. Once you're tucked up in bed, I'll show you the picture I painted while you and Mummy were having your picnic.'

True to his word, he brought the painting to let me see. It was still wet, not to be touched. Close up, it was just blobs of colour. When Dad held it against the wall, I could see a rocky sea scene with gulls and waves and two orange sailing boats.

*

Yes, Mariella, I thought, I remember when that picture of yours was painted. But where? Try as I might, I couldn't bring the place to mind. And why is it hanging in your house? How do you come into my story? Tomorrow, I thought, as I fell over the edge of sleep, tomorrow I'm going to get on with a bit of detective work. Just as well it's Saturday.

I woke in the night, mid-dream, to the sound of thunder, rain cascading down the window and zigzags of lightning tearing the sky like scissors across silk. My heart was pounding. 'Are you all right, Lucy-girl?' I heard Nan call.

She plodded into my bedroom. 'Hot chocolate?' she asked. 'Just the answer to a night like this, although to be sure, the garden needs rain.'

We sat, elbows on the kitchen table, hands clasping our mugs, like old school friends settling down for a gossip. Nan was such a comforting person, I reflected. All through my childhood, when things got difficult at home, I knew I could rely on her. I broached what might prove to be a tricky subject. 'Nan, I'd like to go home tomorrow,' I said.

'Home? To stay?' She looked a shade alarmed.

'No, just to look round, pick up the mail, some clothes,

that kind of thing.' That wasn't the exact truth, but it was close.

'D'you want me to come with you?'

'No thanks, Nan. I'll be fine on my own.'

Nan looked me in the eye. She didn't fuss. That was another of her good points. 'Take your mobile – and make sure it's switched on,' was all she said. She kissed me and went upstairs. 'I won't be long behind you,' I promised.

I tried to make plans, but unsolved puzzles whirled, merry-go-round-style in my head. There was the uncomfortable mystery about Dad, now I couldn't even be sure about Mum any more. These days my whole life is one enormous tangle, I thought.

By the time I got back into bed, the storm had died down, leaving rain to sluice over the outside world, trying in one night to make up for the baking heat of the last few weeks. I wondered how Mum was coping with the weather.

Had the storm wakened her as she lay in her high hospital bed? Had she been frightened and cried out for Dad? Thunder and lightning had always freaked her out. I can remember her lying stretched out on the sofa with a cushion over her head, obviously terrified, pleading with Dad to make it go away.

'I'm scared, Charlie...' I saw him wince at the pet name, 'make the naughty noise stop. Please, Charlie, please!'

'Don't fuss, darling. You'll frighten Lucy if you're not careful. Shh! There's a good girl...' as though she was about four years old herself.

I thought of her as I'd seen her earlier today, such a tiny figure covered with a blue blanket, her breathing rasping in and out to the pattern of a green trace on the wall. Plumbed into a variety of tubes and bags, she looked very vulnerable.

'Is my mum going to die?' I'd asked the sister.

'Not if I can help it,' she'd said briskly, putting a thermometer gadget into Mum's ear. She had gathered up her notes and disappeared down the corridor.

'Mum, Mum, can you hear me? It's Lucy.' But she had drifted off. 'I love you a lot, honestly, I do,' I said. And, despite everything, I meant it. I stroked the back of her hand. She didn't seem to care, didn't move, didn't say a word. That's when I made up my mind to do something about it. I've got to find out who you are, I thought, then I might discover who I am too. Not knowing was getting to me.

*

Next morning, the sun shone again, as though it had been polished in the night. I was on the point of leaving Nan's when my mobile sang its silly tune. Millie. She went straight to the point, as usual. 'You might have died and gone to heaven for all I've seen of you lately. You still at your Nan's? I'm coming over. No ifs, no buts,' she said.

'Hang on,' I said. 'I'll meet you at my house in half an hour. I'm going to pick up stuff.'

'OK, see you,' Millie said and rang off.

I realised how pleased I was to be meeting Millie. I'd

missed her. She was part of the BDD life, part of the BBC life too, come to that. And, if I'm honest, I wasn't too unhappy to have someone with me in the empty house. Not that I'm a scaredy cat, but it would be reassuring to have the no-nonsense Millie at my side.

I turned the Yale key and pushed open the front door. The stained glass cast its usual blobs of coloured light on the hall floor, like sucked-on fruit gums I used to think when I was little. The house smelled stale, not the way it used to at all. BDD, there was always a welcoming smell of polish, a whiff of antiseptic, and the oily scent of wet paint. If Mum was feeling up to it, which wasn't often, a smell of baking wafted from the kitchen. ADD you could only detect toothpaste, loo freshener and the sad smell of illness.

'Yuk,' said Millie, screwing up her nose. We moved the mountain of mail, special offers, catalogues, bills, the odd get-well card for Mum. I riffled through them, sorting them into piles, while Millie mooched about the living room. 'Let's open a window,' she suggested. We tried, but they were stuck tight.

I wandered into the kitchen. It was as though I'd never been there before. It neither had the right smell nor the proper feel about it. The AGA was cold. The fridge purred, and the clock ticked, but somehow the room was out of kilter, two-dimensional, like a kitchen in a television programme.

*

It was difficult to believe that this was where we used to have breakfast, the three of us – Dad snatching toast, Mum spooning her favourite honey yoghurt, me making milk puddles in my Cornflakes – or worse, being force-fed sticky grey porridge.

One morning, as Mum tried to push a spoonful of the disgusting stuff into my mouth, Dad intervened. Usually, my behaviour was Mum's sole province, but now and again he put his foot down. 'Leave it, Grace,' he said. 'You'll make the child sick.'

'But porridge is good for her,' Mum protested, before flouncing off in tears. She did a marvellous flounce at one time, my mum did – and couldn't stand it if Dad put his oar in. He tipped the offending gloop down the sink, looked at his watch and went racing off after Mum to calm her down.

'Darling, I'm sorry,' he said, taking the stairs two at a time.

'Sorry, you're cross? Sorry, you shouted at me?' I knew she'd be pouting like a China doll as she said it. In those days Mum could make a tremendous fuss about the smallest thing.

'Yes, Grace, sorry I was cross.' No doubt he was by this time. 'Now, I've simply got to get going – a list of visits as long as my arm. Come on, love,' I heard him say. 'Lucy can have Cornflakes or something.'

He kissed me briefly, picked up his case and made for the door. 'Be a good girl for Mummy, Poppet. See you later.'

I don't remember anything more being said, but I was never offered porridge for breakfast again. I learned to take this kind of thing in my stride. Sometimes Mum regressed to her little-girl mode and I just accepted it. Well, you do. You only get one set of parents and have to make the best of it.

Somewhere along the line, however, she changed completely. She got rid of her entire wardrobe of girly clothes and started taming her unruly hair. My recent memories are of a severe, unbending woman, strict towards me, but treating dad with a mixture of withering scorn and dog-like devotion. What on earth happened? Something catastrophic certainly – could it have been the Mariella thing?

*

Millie and I sat at the kitchen table. I found an unopened bottle of Fanta and two glasses. 'Can you keep a secret?' I asked.

Millie's eyes widened to round O's. 'What do you take me for?' she said.

'You see, I need to find out a few things about my mum,' I started. I wasn't ready to talk about my dad, even to Millie, not yet anyway. 'She's proving to be a very mysterious lady.'

'You could have fooled me,' Millie commented, obviously thinking about the hard-boiled buttoned-up woman she knew. 'She seems pretty straightforward to me. But she's your mum…'

You'd be surprised, I thought, but said aloud, 'I need to look for old photographs, letters, school reports, things like that. You won't believe this, but I don't know what she looked like as a child – what school she went to, even where she lived…' I tailed off, the idea of poking through my mother's bits and pieces seemed indecent, somehow.

Millie was made of sterner stuff. 'Where do you keep the black bags?' she asked. She intended to make a proper job of it.

*

'Oh no,' I said. 'We mustn't get rid of anything. Pile the interesting stuff on the table and we'll put everything else back where it came from.'

'OK, you're the boss. Now, where do we start?' She crossed to the cabinet that stood directly beneath one of dad's landscapes, not that she took any notice of the painting, of course. People don't.

'These drawers look promising,' Millie said, opening the top one. But it was empty – bare, clean, dustless. And the rest were the same.

'Do you think anyone's been in here? Burglars maybe?'

'Unlikely – everything's so neat. Nothing's been disturbed. It's just tidy. All Mum's doing, I expect.' *Of course,* I added to myself.

It was strange. We didn't come across a single letter, no photographs, not even one of me as a baby, nothing. I knew that Mum had gone mad after Dad's death, but I didn't think she'd been this efficient. I'd managed to scotch the skip idea, so where had everything gone? Photographs and personal things were of no interest to Oxfam or places like that.

'Not a shred of evidence,' Millie said, in her best TV detective manner. 'Not to worry. Let's look upstairs.'

I felt like a burglar, tiptoeing into Mum's bedroom. With its pale green curtains closed against the sunshine, it was like walking underwater. I shivered. Millie, however, was raring to go.

We began with the dark wood chest of drawers by Mum's bedside. Nothing out of the ordinary, just the usual tights, knickers, bras and a bundle of neatly-ironed cotton handkerchiefs, all very orderly, all totally unexciting, except for a green silk nightdress, so new that it still had its label attached – and a silver fish on a tattered green ribbon.

'Look at this,' Millie said, holding out the pretty silver pendant. 'Try it on.' She looped the ribbon round my neck. I opened the curtains a crack and the fish gleamed in the sun as I moved.

'I've never seen this before,' I said. 'Mum never wore jewellery.'

I undid one of the handkerchiefs. White cotton, edged with lace, a bunch of heather embroidered in the corner. 'Real handkerchiefs, one of Mum's little treats,' I said, refolding it.

'Treat?' Millie scoffed. 'Sounds more like a fetish to me. Everyone in the world uses tissues.'

We looked in the wardrobe, no surprises there, just several dull brown dresses with narrow belts and pleated skirts, so unfashionable it wasn't true. The dresses hung in plastic shrouds, matching jackets on hangers and underneath, brown leather shoes with shoe-trees in.

On the dressing table lay three mirrors, a set of brushes, a nail buffer, a button hook – for pity's sake, who else would own a button hook? – all with matching ribbed green-glass backs. 'What on earth is this for?' asked Millie, holding up the chamois pad thingy.

'It's for polishing your nails. Look,' I said, demonstrating how Mum used to make her nails shine. 'Just as well she's not here to see me fiddling around with her precious brushes and things. She'd have a fit if she knew I'd moved them one centimetre from their allotted spot.'

'This sort of stuff went out with the ark,' Millie said. 'She's out of her time, your mum.'

That's it, I thought. Millie's put her finger on it. My mother doesn't belong in the modern world. I remember when Dad bought the green dressing set from a downtown antique shop, Mum had sounded really excited for once. 'It's like inheriting a family heirloom,' she'd said, placing each item on the dressing table with exaggerated care. 'As if it's been handed down from mother to daughter.'

Not that she ever used the brushes, of course. Well, you couldn't. The pale ancient bristles wouldn't have made it through Mum's thick springy curls. She had a cheap plastic supermarket brush for that job.

Like the drawing room, Mum's bedroom was a dead loss. So too were the kitchen and bathroom. Everything was bland, cleared away, empty of the woman who had lived here all these years, no smell, no clues, no surprises, just the little silver fish which hardly counted.

And there was little sign of Dad either. Not even in the guest bedroom where, for a long time, he had slept. He had been completely banished from sight, as though all his possessions had been cremated alongside his body.

Thank goodness, my bedroom was still in its own untidy state, just as it had been when Mum had her accident. It was a friendly place, with its half-done drawings, books left open on their faces, T-shirts and jeans draped on the back of the chair, Dafyd the dragon, balding teddies and Beanie dolls lined up against the wall.

Millie and I slumped side by side on my bed. 'What's next?' she asked.

'Search me.' I felt defeated. There were no secrets, after all. I didn't know what exactly I was looking for, but I'd been sure I'd find something.

'Do you think your mum's got a thing about photos?' Millie asked, putting my own suspicions into words. 'She seems to have done a pretty thorough job of clearing up. Maybe she guessed you would search the house.'

I played with the pendant; its slim silver fish shape unfamiliar under my fingers. Then, a brainwave!

'Hang on a minute, there's one photograph I bet she's missed,' I said, leaping off the bed to root about at the back of my wardrobe. There, under a pile of outgrown sweaters, was a picture of a young-looking Dad smiling out from a silver frame. I picked it up and smiled back at him.

'I found it face-down on the guest room window sill after Dad died. I managed to smuggle it upstairs before it got black-bagged along with the rest of the stuff.' I dropped the photograph on the bed.

'Hey look,' Millie said, 'the little clip thing at the back has come undone.'

CHAPTER FIVE

I fiddled with the frame, trying to put the photograph back, but it came to pieces in my hand. 'Watch the glass,' Millie warned.

Out from behind Dad's photograph, fluttered a scrap of folded paper. Conscious of Millie breathing over my shoulder, I undid it slowly. It had been so obviously concealed that I was fearful of what I might find. But I needn't have been. It was a pencil sketch on headed notepaper, *Badpenny House, Llyncelyn* – a hotel or a B&B, I suppose.

The drawing was of my mother – and she looked wonderful. It showed her dancing among trees bent over by the wind, the sea in the distance. And she was completely naked, except for a circle of leaves in her hair. Or was it seaweed? rushes? Some kind of greenery, I couldn't quite make it out. She was wearing a pendant – the silver fish? I couldn't be sure. She was holding ribbons in her outstretched hands and looked no more than eighteen or so.

Dad's work, of course, there was no doubt about that, although just a preliminary sketch, done at speed. In his handwriting were notes with arrows, *'sun-streaked'* he had noted of her hair, *'green'* the flying ribbons, *'backlit'* of the dancing figure itself. I knew this was the way he worked - I had watched him do this kind of thing many times before he started on his landscape paintings. Thinking back, I couldn't remember him ever doing figure work, but he was brilliant at it. In a few pencil strokes, he had captured the wonderful fluid movement of the dancer, her flying curls, her pensive mood, her youth. She looked totally unselfconscious, simply concentrating on what she was doing.

'Who on earth…?' Millie could contain her curiosity no longer.

'Mum, of course.'

'Your mum? Let's have a closer look.' She took quite a bit of convincing. 'Wow, if it's her, she was stunning in her day.'

'I wonder…' I said, 'I wonder if Llyncelyn is where Mariella's picture was painted?'

'You've lost me this time,' Millie said. 'Who the blazes is Mariella?'

But I couldn't bear to start on the Mariella saga at that point. 'A sort of lost relative, well, lost and found. I'll tell you about her sometime, I promise.'

'Talk about your mum being a mysterious person – you're not doing too badly in that department yourself,' Millie grumbled. 'Have we finished then?'

'Just the loft,' I said, suddenly terrified that we had left it too late. What if Mum had cleared it too? What about Dad's paintings? She had been determined to get rid of them – and she'd been on her own a lot of the time.

'Ready?' I asked.

'I love attics.' Millie breathed. 'I wrote a poem once, *'The Charm of Attics'* or something like that. I got a B+ for it, I remember.'

'I didn't realise you were such a romantic,' I giggled. 'I'd forgotten that Millie was a poet, always top in our English set. School, and all its ramifications, had sunk to the bottom of my mind these days.

I hadn't been near the loft since Mum's accident. We opened the trapdoor and pulled down the steps. I prayed that she hadn't had time to tamper with Dad's pictures before she fell. She hated that bit of his life so much that I wouldn't put it past her to take a knife to the lot.

Trouble was, the light wasn't working. 'I'll get a torch,' I said, pretty sure that I'd find one hanging from its hook in the hall cupboard. The door appeared to be jammed and I had to wrench it open. Not surprising – it was crammed full of charity bags. So that's where she hid everything! Secrets galore in here, I thought.

'Find it?' Millie's voice floated down.

I grabbed the torch from its usual hook and dashed upstairs, promising to come back sometime and do the bags on my own.

'You first,' Millie said.

I climbed the ladder, taking each step with care.
Millie followed.

'Watch you don't put your foot through the rafters. Keep to the floorboards,' I warned. In the torchlight, the loft was an eerie place. The skylight had been covered with black paper, so it took a few minutes for our eyes to get used to the shadowy dimness.

Gradually, things took shape. Easels propped on their sides, legs sticking out, paintings stacked face to the wall, a palette with hardened paint looking like dried flower heads, tubes and rags, charcoal and brushes – all the paraphernalia of the artist. This was my Dad's kingdom. And it was just as he'd left it. I breathed a sigh of relief.

Relief didn't last long. 'Listen! There's someone in the house,' I whispered.

We heard the unmistakable sound of footsteps on the stairs, climbing slowly, ever so slowly… plod, plod, plod.

We stood rooted, looking down. We didn't scream.

'Hi, anyone up there?' Then the ladder creaked and Henry's face loomed up through the trapdoor.

'Henry, you idiot!' I was furious.

'The front door was standing open,' Henry said with exasperating reasonableness. 'Your Nan said I'd find you here. I've brought you a present, well, a kind of present.' And he held out a supermarket bag.

Bless Nan, practical Nan. She had sent Henry round with our lunch. Now that we were reminded of it, we were starving. 'My stomach thinks it's stuck to my back,' Millie said.

We sat around the kitchen table, eating chicken sandwiches, crisps and biscuits, a cross between a picnic and a party. Millie could hardly keep her eyes off Henry. 'Where did you find him?' she signalled. I put my finger to my lips. Henry was one of my secrets – and, as I already seemed to be sharing him with Mariella, Millie hadn't a hope.

'Any further on?' Henry asked.

'Not a lot,' I admitted. 'But we've found heaps of Dad's paintings stacked in the attic.'

'I wouldn't mind ferreting around among them one day,' Henry said.

'I'll keep you to that,' I said, as my mobile trilled into life. It was Nan reminding me that I'd need to be back to get my things together for my afternoon visit to the hospital.

I gathered up Dad's photograph, the sketch and all the post that looked important and locked up. I turned to find that Henry had sprung another of his surprises. He was holding open the back door of an ancient Cortina. 'Want a lift?' he asked.

I saw that Millie had wasted no time. She was already ensconced in the front passenger seat. 'Thanks,' I said. 'How long have you had this?'

'Not mine,' Henry said. 'It's on a long loan – the guy who owns my flat lets me use it. It's no great shakes, but it goes.'

Henry dropped Millie off first. 'Thanks, Mill,' I said. I'll see you on Monday, worse luck.'

'No problem,' she said, making a 'you-lucky-so-and-so' face behind Henry's back. 'I enjoyed it.'

'I'll drive you to the Heath if you like,' Henry offered, puffed up with pride, so I took him up on it and he pottered about, making polite conversation with Nan, while I got everything ready.

'Can't hang around,' Henry said. 'The parking's impossible on a Saturday afternoon. Tell you what, call me when you're finished and I'll come back for you. By the way, you wouldn't have a couple of quid towards the petrol, would you?'

Henry, the hero, I thought, handing over my bus fare. Typical.

*

Mum was sitting out in a high-backed chair, no longer hooked up to the monitor above the bed. She looked much more with it. 'You've had your hair done,' I said. 'Looks lovely.' And it did, shiny and pulled back into a ponytail.

'Jenny, one of the nurses, did it,' she said. 'I've got to get back into the swing of things, they say. But it's the tiredness, you wouldn't believe, Lucy.' Great, she knows it's me, I thought.

I put her clean things into the locker, gave her a get-well card to open, a plastic spoon and a jar of fresh raspberries in sugar. She seemed pleased, whether it was seeing me or the bits and pieces I'd brought from the outside world, I didn't know.

I perched on the edge of the bed while she started on the raspberries. The pendant gleamed in the sun. I'd clean forgotten I was wearing it. Mum stretched out her hand and touched the silver fish. She looked me straight in the eye. Here it comes, I thought. She'll know I've been through her things. She'll go mad. But no, not this time.

'You're not supposed to be wearing this, not yet,' she said

quietly.

'I'm sorry, Mum. It's so pretty...' I hunted around for a feasible excuse. But she wasn't fazed.

'That fish came from a place by the sea,' she said. 'I was there too, when I was very small, just a child. I can't quite remember...' She looked lost in thought, like she'd gone far away inside her head. Then, brightening, 'We went back there once, your dad and me, before you came along.'

A shot in the dark. 'Llyncelyn?' I asked.

'Yes, that's it. Llyncelyn,' she repeated, conversationally. 'That's where the Daughters of Awar live.' It was hard to follow the thread.

'The daughters of Awar? From the Mabinogion?'

This time I'd lost Mum completely. 'From a storybook? No, the Daughters of Awar are real, as real as you and me. They look after foundlings, you know, girls, no boys, just girls.'

'Like an orphanage?' Things might be about to fall into place. 'You were one of the orphans, Mum?'

She looked most offended. 'Not me. I was no orphan. I had a mother, you know. Once. I must have one, stands to reason, everyone has a mother. Not that I ever knew who she was...' And she began to cry, a quiet kind of crying, tears rolling silently down her cheeks. Dad had always warned me against probing into her past. Now I knew why.

Out of the blue, she went on. 'They taught the girls to dance, I remember.'

'You were a dancer too, Mum, weren't you?'

'Not me,' Mum said emphatically. 'I've never been a dancer. What gave you that idea? Grace is the most unsuitable name for someone like me – I've got lead in my feet – can't dance, never could.'

I was struggling. I had Dad's picture tucked at the bottom of my bag to prove that she had once danced with fantastic grace. But this wasn't the most appropriate time to produce it.

I gave her one of the clean handkerchiefs. She sniffed a bit, gathered herself together and announced, 'I'm married to a doctor, you know. I am Grace White, the doctor's wife.'

'Yes, Mum, I know. He was my dad.'

'Your dad?' Mum gazed at me as though she'd never met me before. 'No,' she said. 'I don't think so.'

I didn't know whether to laugh or cry. In the end, I resorted to anger. 'Stop it, Mum. Remember me? I'm Lucy, your daughter. Yours and Dad's.'

Mum had lost interest in the conversation by this time. 'I'm tired,' she complained. 'I need to get back to bed.' I helped her out of her dressing gown, tidied the pillows and watched her clamber into the high bed. I covered her with a blanket and tiptoed away. I didn't know whether she was asleep or not – and frankly, I didn't much care.

'I'll see you again tomorrow, Mum,' I promised wearily, bundling yesterday's washing into a plastic bag. Defeated, I kissed her on the forehead and stumbled out of the ward.

I arranged to meet Henry outside the hospital gates, cheered by the thought of talking sense to someone. 'How is she?' he asked.

'Awful, simply awful,' I said. 'Sometimes she hasn't a clue who I am – and as for Dad, she was banging on about him again. Henry, I can't stand it. I don't know what to do.'

'What about your Nan? Can't she help?'

'Not really. Mum and Nan are oil and water.' I was silent for a while, thinking, just thinking. In less than a year my life had turned upside down and inside out. I sighed, searching for a more exciting topic than Mum's weirdness.

'Ever heard of the Daughters of Awar?' I asked. Worth a try, I thought. Henry is one of those people you'd want on your side in a pub quiz. He can come up with the right answer to the most unlikely questions.

Not this time, though. He shook his head. 'But I know a man who does.'

We drove back the way we'd come, scorching round a roundabout and through a maze of downtown streets. We stopped outside the library, a gloomy high-vaulted building. 'Follow me,' Henry said. He spoke to the guy on the counter and led the way to a bank of computers. He sat down, tapped in his code and in a few minutes, through the magic of the net, *Daughters of Awar* flashed up on the screen.

'Why d'you want to know about this lot?'

'Just something Mum said.' The screen was filled with curly print and symbols of the sea. Mysterious breathy music flowed from the speakers.

'Interesting,' Henry said, peering at the computer. 'It looks like some kind of a cult – white witches and things.'

'Not an orphanage?'

'Most certainly not. It's got all sorts of stuff about meditation and magic rituals.'

My mouth went dry with excitement. 'Can you find out what they do?'

'They seem to do a lot of dancing. Naked,' Henry added, warming to his theme. 'And they make sacrifices to the god of the sea...'

'To Neptune?'

'Not Neptune, Dylan – the Welsh sea god,' Henry said, eyes glued to the computer. 'It says here that their celebration rituals take the form of dance and song. Does your mum sing?'

'No, but she used to dance, although she says she can't remember much about it. Hey, what's this?' A picture of a fish had come up on the screen, beneath it an explanatory note, saying it was an emblem of Dylan himself. 'Look,' I showed Henry the silver fish pendant that I'd tucked under my T-shirt.

'That's it exactly!' he shouted, matching it to the on-screen version. The other browsers shushed him. 'Sorry, he whispered. 'Let's do a print-out and get going.'

I scanned it quickly as soon as we got back to the car. 'There's masses of stuff about *'Wiccan'* and *'magic'* here,' I said. 'It all looks dead serious.'

'Dead dodgy, more like,' Henry said. 'You mean that your mother was somehow mixed up with the Daughters of Awar? Sounds highly unlikely. How do you know?'

'I don't,' I said. 'But I've got three clues, one, Dad told Nan she'd been tickled by witches – I thought it was just a figure of speech – now I'm beginning to wonder. Two, this necklace, which Millie and I found hidden in Mum's drawer, but I don't ever remember seeing her wear it,' I touched the silver fish, 'and three, promise you won't tell, look at this.' And I gave the Henry the torn and taped-up pencil sketch.

'Good God,' he said. 'What a figure!'

'Put your eyeballs back in, Henry, and concentrate,' I laughed, 'you know the picture that Mariella showed me …'

'The seaside thing?'

'Yes. I'm almost sure it was painted at Llyncelyn.'

'And Llyncelyn is where the Daughters of Awar hang out?'

'You've got it, Henry. Got it in one… '

'So, what are we waiting for?' Henry switched on the engine. 'There's a map in the back seat,' he said.

'Hold on. What about Nan? I can't just disappear.'

'Tell her I'm taking you out for a meal,' he suggested.

'She'll never believe that. You never have any cash – you even had to borrow money for petrol, don't forget.'

'I'm relying on you to have a couple of tenners tucked away in your bag.'

'You know me too well, Henry Davies,' I said, as I scrolled down to Nan's number. I felt a bit ashamed when all Nan said was that after putting up with an old bat like her, I deserved time out with people of my own age.

CHAPTER SIX

We chattered almost non-stop as we gobbled up the miles, like getting to know one another again. Henry had once been a more or less permanent fixture in my life – in the BDD days, of course.

'Anything going on between you and Mariella?' I felt able to ask as we got nearer West Wales.

'Not that much,' Henry said. 'I try to keep an eye on her – she's got a lot on her plate at the moment. You've got your grandma around, she's all on her own.'

'Her mum's not back then?'

'No, she's working away. Keeping her mind off your dad's death, I expect.'

'What's my dad's death got to do with her anyway?' I asked, beginning to feel angry at this unknown woman laying claim to my private grief.

'Everything,' I heard Henry say quietly, as he drew up at a Little Chef. Over a cup of coffee – all we could afford between us – Henry said, 'Mariella wants you to have this. I meant to let you see it earlier, but with Millie there…' Handing me a well-thumbed photograph, his words dried up.

It was a picture of my nan, looking a lot younger, with a baby in her arms. The baby had a fuzz of fair hair and huge solemn eyes. She was a chubby little girl in blue cord dungarees. Her bare toes curled like seashells. My nan, yes – but the baby wasn't me.

I turned it over. On the back, in Dad's handwriting, it read *Mariella, six months.*

'I'd almost forgotten,' I breathed. I'd been so tied up in finding out about mum's past, that I'd almost forgotten about the dad and Mariella business. 'She really is my sister... '

'Half-sister,' Henry, ever the pedant, pointed out. 'Your nan doesn't know she's back living a couple of streets away, so don't let on.'

It was all getting a bit much. This time last week I didn't know Mariella existed, now I had to share her with not only my Dad and Henry, but Nan as well. I slumped down in my seat. The West Wales adventure was fast beginning to lose its sparkle.

'Aren't you supposed to be map-reading?' Henry said, 'Because we're not far now, I reckon. We don't want to miss the turning.'

And sure enough, it said LLYNCELYN, large as life on the next signpost. The village looked so ordinary in the evening sunlight, with its corner shop, chapel and kiddies' playground, that all thoughts of *Wiccan* and *magic* seemed the stuff of nightmares.

It was shaping up to be the longest day of my life. I said as much to Henry.

He looked at his watch. 'Come to think, this *is* the longest day – of the year, I mean.'

'Feels like it too.' Without thinking, I grabbed Henry's hand. He didn't object. Henry's not the sexiest thing on two legs,

I thought, but he's good to have around. 'Let's make the most of it,' I said.

'Like what?' Henry sounded a tad apprehensive.

'Like explore Llyncelyn now that we're here, maybe go for a paddle and smell the sea.' I was back in full-on adventure mode. We strolled along the cliff path, looking down on waves purring up the beach. It was a beautiful evening.

*

'Stop, Henry!' I had the oddest feeling. 'I'm certain this is where Dad did Mariella's painting.'

'Sure?'

'Almost.'

We hesitated, gazing at the scene below us. I saw the cove, the rocks and a stretch of sand just as I remembered them – only the orange sailing boats were missing – and, in my imagination, I saw dad sitting on a rock, sea pinks making a comfortable cushion, painting kit open by his side.

'If I'm right, I've been to this place too,' I told Henry. 'Just once, when I was quite little.' I thought about that dreadful picnic with Mum and shuddered.

'We're supposed to be here for a purpose,' Henry reminded me. 'You haven't forgotten?'

'Of course not.' We stood silent, just taking it all in. Tonight wasn't the raw seascape of Dad's painting, it was pure tranquillity.

'What now?' Henry turned his back on the view.

'Let's see if we can find their old B&B, what was it called? *Halfpenny House?'*

We walked along a clifftop path, listening to the lazy sound of waves splashing over the rocks below. The sun still held most of its daytime heat. We took it slowly, reading aloud the names of the guest houses as we passed. *Gull's Way, Ty Hafen, Grey Gables.* Thoughts of needles and haystacks came to mind.

Suddenly, we saw it, tucked away behind a high wall, *Badpenny House,* it said on the gatepost. 'That must be it,' I said. *'Bad* not *Half...'* I couldn't believe it was still there, not in its original glory, I imagine, but still more or less in one piece.

'Do you think they might have come here on honeymoon?' Henry asked, looking at the grim grey-stone building, standing well away from the other houses.

'She wouldn't have been waltzing about in the nude then, surely?' That idea didn't quite add up.

'Let's see if they've got a visitors' book.' Henry was off up the path before I could stop him. The hall was dim and shadowy. It didn't look as though the B&B had many guests. Henry rang the brass bell on the desk. An unexpectedly elegant woman with a pelmet of white hair appeared from a door at the back.

'Can I help you?' she asked.

'Well, it's really for my friend...' Henry, lost for words for once, pushed me forward.

'I think my mother and father might have stayed here at

one time – sixteen or more years ago. They were probably on honeymoon…' I was stammering by now. This was a really stupid thing to be doing. 'I'm sorry to bother you,' I began, anxious to make my way back to the front door.

The woman looked surprised. 'Your mother was here? Sure?'

'I don't really know,' I said, in full retreat by this time. 'I just wondered. It's probably a mistake.'

She came close, so close I could see my reflection in her oval spectacles. 'Hold on, I think I recognise you, my dear.' She peered at me for what seemed like a full minute. 'Grace's daughter? Right?'

Before I could answer, she reached out to touch the silver fish on the ribbon at my neck. 'Poor child,' she said. 'I'm so sorry. So you're a child of Awar now too. Come in, my dear. You must tell us what happened.' She lifted the hem of her long green skirt, came out into the hall and took me by the hand. Her hand was smooth and cold, cold as the sea. I wanted to refuse but found myself being propelled through the dark door.

'Henry!' I called in panic. 'Henry!'

'Don't worry,' he said placidly. 'I'll wait in the car for you.' He raised a hand in salute and disappeared into the evening sunlight.

*

'We've been expecting you – or your mother. Every daughter comes back eventually,' the woman in green said. 'They all come back like bad…'

'Like bad pennies,' I said.

'Exactly,' she agreed. 'You're a bright girl. Do you dance?'

'I've never danced in my life,' I said 'But I think my mother did.'

'Well, of course,' said the woman. 'All the daughters of Awar are dancers.'

She guided me into a room at the back of the house where there must have been a dozen others, all women, chatting to one another and smiling. They were all wearing green. Apart from that, no two were alike. Skinny women, tubby women, mostly elderly, although I caught sight of another girl about my own age.

'Sainsbury's,' I overheard one of the older women say, 'quite the best for organic vegetables.'

'Yes,' her neighbour agreed. 'but Tesco's aren't bad either.'

'A lot of gossips, we are,' my elderly guide said. 'It's a long time since your dear mother was with us. My name is Rhiannon,' she held out her cool hand, 'and you are?'

'Lucy.'

'Well Lucy, welcome. Sit by me and tell us what has happened to Grace.' The talking had died down. Everyone was listening.

'She's in hospital…'

'When did she pass on?'

'Do you mean *die?*' I squealed, horrified. 'She's got cancer, but they're treating it. I saw her just this afternoon. She can't be dead, she was eating raspberries and talking about Llyncelyn…' I couldn't go on. 'Anyway, what makes you think she's dead?'

'The fish, my dear. You're wearing the silver fish.' I looked around. Each woman had a silver fish at her throat. 'It's a sign,' Rhiannon explained. 'It means that you are motherless, as is every daughter of Awar.' She swept an arm around the room.

I yanked at the thin green ribbon. It broke and the fish rattled to the floor. 'I found it in Mum's drawer,' I said. 'I don't want to wear it, not if it means my mum is dead.' At this moment, my stern difficult mother became very precious and, more than anything, I wanted her alive.

'I thought we hadn't seen the white raven,' one of the others said. 'I know my eyesight isn't what it was, but I'm sure I wouldn't have missed him.'

'White raven?' I repeated. 'Is it important?'

'When a mother dies, the white raven flies…' she said, obviously quoting some rhyme. I shivered at the very idea.

Rhiannon picked up the silver fish. 'Put it away safely until you need it,' she said. I shoved it deep into my bag. It came to rest beside Dad's pencil sketch. Never mind ravens, I thought to myself, think pigeons, like putting a cat among them. I took out the drawing, unfolded it carefully and, without a word, handed it to Rhiannon.

'It's Grace,' she breathed. 'She should have destroyed this.'

The women crowded round. 'Still, it's incredibly beautiful,' one said.

'Beautiful, yes. But she should have torn it up. It's the rules.'

I grabbed it back before anyone could damage it. They wouldn't have recognised the Grace of the past few years.

'You know the artist?' Rhiannon asked.

'My dad,' I said. 'I found the drawing this morning, hidden away beside this photograph.' Had it just been this morning? It felt like a lifetime away.

'I hope there are no more pictures,' one old woman said.

'I don't think so. My Nan says Mum got rid of her other portraits.'

'Indeed I should hope so.' The old woman began to chant in a high reedy voice. It went something like this,

'Bad luck to those who our spirits steal,
No magic words will their black hearts heal.'

*

I didn't know what she was on about, but it sounded terribly sinister. All I wanted was to be back in the outside world with Henry. But they wouldn't let me go, not yet anyway.

The old lady, conscious of her audience, went into storytelling mode. 'One winter's night,' she began, 'when snow lay deep on the ground, the white raven flew over the trees, there, just there.' She pointed to the woods beyond the garden. 'The raven swooped past the windows, up towards the moon and back, again and again, until at last we took notice.' You could feel a shiver rippling around the listening women.

'We couldn't ignore him, so two or three of us younger ones – we were young once, you know – bundled up warm and followed him. The raven led us to a snow-filled hollow and there she was, a tiny baby wrapped in a green silk shawl.' She turned to me. 'That baby was your mother. She looked like a chrysalis, but she had a lusty yell, so we knew there wasn't much wrong with her.'

'There was a note tucked into the shawl,' another grey-haired woman chipped in. 'It had just one word on it, in beautiful Gothic script. It said, **GRACE**.'

'And, in her little fist, clutched tight, was a silver fish – the very one you were wearing when you arrived,' Rhiannon said. I was very glad I'd taken it off. What if there's a spell on it? Don't let them get to you, I told myself.

'So you took the baby in?'

'She was one of us, the fish proved it, the youngest daughter we've ever had with us …'

'And the most beautiful.'

It made me a bit sad, thinking about the motherless child my mum had been. No wonder she got twitchy when relatives were mentioned. Being a foundling was enough to spook anyone.

Rhiannon saw my look. 'Don't be too sorry for her,' she

said. 'We were all besotted with Grace. We spoiled her rotten, I used to think. She had lots of mothers, after all, and everyone wanted a turn.' But she had never known her real mother, someone of her very own, someone to cuddle up to or get mad at. Maybe I was just beginning to understand what had been eating her all those years.

'Did you ever meet my dad?' I asked. In for a penny, in for a pound, I thought.

'We did. Indeed, we did,' Rhiannon said grimly.

*

It turned out that Nan didn't have the whole story. Dad hadn't met Mum in the art class. He'd met her here in Llyncelyn where he'd stopped to do some painting. Apparently he had come across her dancing on the clifftop and been so bewitched by her beauty that he followed her back to Badpenny House. Then they slipped out to be with one another day after day.

'Your father painted her picture over and over again. He encouraged her to renounce her vows and we can never forgive him that,' Rhiannon said.

'We couldn't persuade her to stay, no matter how hard we tried,' another old woman added. 'She insisted she'd met the love of her life and nothing would do but to go back with him to the big city.'

'It was so wrong of her – an artist, of all things!'

'My father was a doctor,' I said.

'That's as may be, but he stole Grace's soul. She only

came back to us once after that. Too little, too late. It was a bad scene for everyone.' Rhiannon folded her lips into a thin line. The story was finished. Time for me to go.

Anyway, I'd had enough and could scarcely keep my eyes open. Images were shimmying around in my head. 'Thank you for telling me Mum's story,' I managed.

Rhiannon caught me by the shoulders. 'You can't go yet. Don't you know it's the longest day?' I did, courtesy of Henry, but I didn't see what that had to do with anything.

The women stood up slowly, making a circle around me. The youngest one grabbed hold of my hands. Hers were icy cold. 'We celebrated the summer solstice at sun-up this morning. And tonight, at sun-down, we mark its close.' I must have looked completely blank. 'Don't you know anything?' she asked. 'On this, the longest day, we honour Dylan, the sea god.'

'Not me,' I said. 'It's getting pretty late and…'

'Yes, you especially Lucy.' Rhiannon was most insistent. 'After all, you were wearing Dylan's sacred symbol.' Not now, I'm not. Never again, if I've got anything to do with it, I resolved.

'Sounds very interesting,' I said, 'but…'

They crowded me, kindly, but with a certain menace. I had to escape from this crowd of batty women. If I can reach the loo, I'll text Henry, I thought. Even that proved impossible. There was no signal. I hope he's been in touch with Nan, I thought, beginning to panic.

The young girl was extremely bossy. 'Get your things off

quickly,' she said, yanking my T-shirt over my head. 'No time to waste.' She gave me a long silky robe to put on, green of course, and put a wreath of sticky seaweed round my head. It smelled horrible.

'Must I?'

'You must. You came back. They won't let you go,' she said.

'*I* didn't come back,' I argued. 'You're mixing me up with my mother. It's the first time *I've* ever set foot in this place.' And the last, I promised myself.

'That's nit-picking,' she said. 'Lighten up. Enjoy!'

I figured I didn't have much choice. I was herded out into the summer night among the others, all in rustling skirts. I began to understand what my mother had been up against. No wonder she grabbed at the chance to go off with my dad. Henry, where are you? I wondered. I made up my mind to creep away once the so-called celebration had begun.

It was truly weird. The old women puffed and panted as they climbed to the top of the cliff where there was a patch of green, so green it was almost luminous. It was just beyond the wind-bent trees where my dad must have first caught sight of Mum dancing. Once they got their breath back, the women chatted together about the price of butter, how difficult it is to get a good gardener these days, that kind of thing. Then, at some invisible sign, they quietened, settling down on the grass like a flock of bright birds.

They sat in a circle, waiting until the sun sank its great orange disk into the sea. In the last rays of sunlight, they stood up and linked hands, gazing heavenwards, silent and completely still. Everything around them was hushed too. They remained like this for ages, how long it was, I don't know.

When it began to get dark, the silence was broken as though a spell had been lifted. The air was filled once more with the sounds of a summer night, leaves gossiping in the treetops, waves murmuring on the shore, a solitary gull overhead.

The word *magic* must have been invented for what happened next. First the chanting. Pure jargon, as far as I could hear. No wonder Mum went funny.

Then the music. Warbly nose-flute stuff, sounding unearthly as it floated between the trees. To my surprise, I saw Rhiannon bend down to change the track on an ancient CD player – nothing magic about that, I thought.

The women began to dance to the music. They swirled and dipped, floating among the shadows like wraiths. Despite myself, I was drawn into the strange ritual and became part of it. Me, Lucy White, who had never tried to dance in her life. If Henry was watching, I knew I'd never live it down. And yet, I hoped he was. He was my only means of escape.

Exhausted, everyone sank down at last on the dampening grass. No wonder they were tired, if all these old dears had been up and doing since dawn. They passed round a sweet drink that tasted like cranberry-flavoured water – I hoped it was nothing more sinister.

I found that I couldn't stay awake for another minute. I drifted off to the murmur of a monotonous song-cum-chant, that went something like, *'Harm ye none, ye daughters of Awar. Be steadfast and endure, ye daughters of Awar...'* And loads more in the same vein. *'Ye daughters of Awar'* came up a lot, like a refrain.

Suddenly, a gong reverberated through the clearing. I woke up in fright, wondering where on earth I was. It was a rude awakening. I found myself being propelled into the middle of a moonlit circle.

'This year, my dear, you are the chosen one, the youngest of us all,' Rhiannon said. 'You have the honour of dancing for the Sea-god. Take the sacred ribbons.' She shoved green ribbons into my hands and ordered me to undress. The youngest girl tried to help me.

'Not me', I said, thoroughly awake and struggling. 'You've made a big mistake. I'm Lucy, not Grace!' I'd got my second wind by now. I hitched the green gown up to my knees and scampered, leaving the celebrants to their own spooky devices. Shoeless, I made for Badpenny House as fast as my legs would take me.

As luck would have it, the door was unlocked. I grabbed my jeans and a top and sprinted along the path towards the town. Praise be, the car was still parked in the same place, Henry dozing behind the wheel.

CHAPTER SEVEN

'Am I glad to see you?' I wheezed as I fell into the passenger seat. 'Quick, get going before they put a spell on us!'

'What kept you?' Henry was ultra-calm. 'Didn't it go too well? Did you find out about your mother? Did they know her?'

'Give me a minute to catch my breath,' I said. 'In order, no, yes and yes.'

'Well then, it was worth it. And I've squared things with your nan. She thinks we've had a puncture and are waiting for the AA.'

'Henry! That's a big fat lie! You're not even a member of the AA. And it's the middle of the night. She'll be out of her mind with worry...'

'OK, Clever Cloggs. You come up with a better idea.'

I couldn't, not on the spur of the moment. 'I'm so hungry,' I said, 'I could eat a horse.' Horses were off the menu, Henry told me, as he passed me the remains of a bar of Dairy Milk, well beyond its sell-by date. I don't even like milk chocolate, but it tasted wonderful.

'So how did it go?' I filled him in as best as I could.

'And the nude dancing? You chickened out?' He considered things for a moment. 'That must have been where you're dad came into the picture – when they got your mum to skip around naked.'

'Lucky my dad was there to rescue her,' I said.

76

Henry drove on into the night, humming some tuneless song to himself. I dozed. At some point in the middle of nowhere, the car slowed down, juddered, and finally gasped to a stop.

'Umm,' said Henry. 'I don't know how to put this to you, but we've run out of petrol.'

'The oldest excuse in the book,' I said.

'Your nan said we shouldn't try to make it back tonight. She thought I'd be too tired to drive.'

'And where are we supposed to be staying?'

'Don't worry. I told her we'd kip down in the back of the car, if necessary. Sorted!' Henry sounded very pleased with himself.

So pleased, in fact, that I started to laugh. It was the kind of laughing where you can't stop, no matter how hard you try. Here we were, on a mad-hatter hunt, stuck for the rest of the night on some lonely B road in West Wales. Nobody would believe it.

Henry sounded bemused. 'What's so funny?' he asked.

'Nothing. Everything,' I spluttered, completely hyped up by this time, I guess. Henry produced a moth-eaten rug from the boot and suggested that we try to get some sleep. He took off his glasses and put them carefully into the glove compartment. It wasn't all that warm, so I snuggled up close to him.

All set for romance? I wondered, but I misread the signs.

'Hey, don't get any ideas…' Henry started. 'It's not that I don't like you Luce. Of course, I do. It's just that I don't really fancy you.'

Good grief, I thought, he's gay. Not Henry. No, 'I've made a date with another girl – and I don't half fancy her!'

'Mariella?'

'No, Millie.'

'Millie!' Fast worker, I thought. 'How did you manage that?' I wanted to know. 'You've only just met her.'

'Through the magic of modern communication,' Henry said with evident satisfaction. 'Mobiles are wonderful things. She gave me her number while you were locking up this morning – and I've had a lot of time to myself this evening.'

It's not that I yearn for old Henry night after night, but it's comforting to know that he's *there!* I began to feel that my whole life was crumbling. Bad enough that I don't know who I am these days, what with Mum and her wacky set of mothers, my non-Dad and my newly out-of-the-woodwork half-sister, without Millie adding to it by pinching the nearest thing to a boyfriend that I possess. If I hadn't felt so sleepy, I'd have stamped my foot with frustration. Life is not fair!

As soon as it was light, we set off to look for a petrol station. Not easy in that part of rural Wales. I was down to my last fiver, so we scraped the bottom of our pockets and the lining of my bag and managed to grub up the best part of £3. Just enough to get us home provided we didn't want to eat.

The garage man took pity on us. 'Out all night? You must be starving.' He gave us a couple of sandwiches, a bag of crisps and a can of Coke. 'On me,' he reassured us. 'What brought you here then?'

As we were his only customers this Sunday morning, he settled down for a good old gossip, elbows on the counter. 'You saw that nutty lot at Llyncelyn?' he said. 'Tell you what, you wouldn't believe the stuff they get up to – or used to, at any rate.' He grew all conspiratorial, his voice dropping to a whisper. 'They say at one time it was open house for the local lads when the youngest girls were feeling randy – mind you, I don't guarantee the truth of it – I never got mixed up with it myself, of course.'

'Any special time of the year?' Henry asked innocently.

'About now, I reckon. They do a lot of their mumbo-jumbo around the longest day.'

We thanked our new-found friend profusely and made our way back to the car, carrying a can of petrol. 'What date's your birthday?' Henry asked me casually.

'21st March. Why? Are you thinking of sending me a card?'

Henry was counting on his fingers. 'Don't you see? It fits,' he said, *'if* your mum went back to the Awar crowd for a summer solstice bash, you could just have been conceived...'

'You mean, one of the 'local lads' could be my father? No, Henry. Absolutely not! I can't – won't – believe it!'

'OK, keep your hair on. But perhaps that was what your mum was getting at. Any way of finding out if she ever went back?'

All of a sudden, it was too much for me. I only wanted to

be back at home with Nan, safe and sound. I no longer felt fifteen years old, more like five. I didn't even know who I was any longer. 'How long will it take to get home?' I asked.

Henry drove steadily. By lunchtime, the Cardiff signs came into view. The A470, the M4 and at last the jewelled streets of Splott. 'Thanks, Henry. Thanks a million.' I aimed a kiss in his general direction. 'Have fun with Millie.' Generous of me, I thought.

'Let me know if anything is happening,' he said. Then, as an afterthought, 'If you're going through your dad's paintings, give me a call. I'll come and help you.' That was Henry all over. With a brief wave, he was gone.

*

Smiling widely, Nan greeted me at the door. 'Back like the proverbial bad penny, I see.'

'Please don't say that, Nan,' I said.

'Why ever not?' I settled down with toast and a boiled egg, a chocolate biscuit and a can of Coke and told her everything I could remember about *Badpenny House* and its weird occupants.

'Where's this silver fish, then?' she asked. I dug it out from the depths of my bag. 'Never laid eyes on it before. Of course, she's not one for jewellery, your mum.'

I looked at the clock. 'I'd better be getting along to the hospital,' I said.

'Now? It's getting late and I don't suppose you feel much

like it.'

'No, but I must. I promised.' What if my wearing the pendant made her go and die? My fault. I couldn't bear it.

'I'll come with you,' Nan offered. 'Just for the ride. I won't come in, although a word with the staff might be a good idea.'

We sat upstairs on the bus. Being Sunday, it wasn't busy. My nan was an easy person to be with. We didn't need to talk all the time, Nan and me – Mariella's nan too, of course. I didn't dare broach that subject at this moment. It could wait.

A comfortable silence. Me, half-asleep, Nan off thinking about things inside her head. Then she said, 'Perhaps that's where your mum went when the Mariella business came to a head.'

'Where?'

'*Badpenny House.*'

Possible, I thought. We knew for a fact that Dad had fallen in love with another woman, Arabella, who was – is – a sculptor. 'Not nearly as beautiful as your mother, of course, but they fell for one another, hook, line and sinker,' Nan said.

'And Mum found out?'

'She went bananas, bonkers,' Nan said. 'Well, you know what she's like. Threatened suicide. It was all over the papers.'

'So what happened?'

'That's the really mysterious bit. She was marched back from wherever she was and nobody has mentioned it from that day to this. It was like it never happened. The next we heard, you were on the way.'

*

We reached our stop. Mum's ward had become something of a second home to me by this time. I had learned the routine and would have recognised its faint Dettol smell a mile off. I knew several of the patients and most of the nurses by name.

'She's been asking for you,' the sister said.

Mum looked like a different person today. For a start, she wasn't alone. Sitting beside the bed, on an upright chair, was a middle-aged man with not a lot in the way of hair, whom I'd never met. Mum was in her most business-like mode, looking completely in charge of the situation, like she sometimes managed in the weeks after Dad died.

'This is my daughter, Lucy,' she said, introducing us. 'This gentleman, Mr Harris, has brought us some good news.' It was a good imitation of her BDD style. I hope it lasts, I thought.

'Pleased to meet you.' The man held out his hand, slimy with perspiration. Despite what he'd said, he looked none too happy, baring yellow teeth in a somewhat fabricated smile.

'Mr Harris found this picture in a junk shop window. He thinks it might be worth something if it's authentic. It's one of your Dad's, isn't it?' For someone who'd never shown the remotest interest in his work when he was alive, Mum sounded very enthusiastic.

Reluctantly, the man undid a newspaper parcel and produced the Llyncelyn seascape I'd last seen at Mariella's. I was so astonished that I said without thinking, 'This picture isn't ours. It belongs to Mariella's mother.'

'Nonsense!' Mum sounded brisk and uncompromising. 'If it's a Charles White, then it's my property,' she said. 'Anyway, I've signed Mr Harris's document, so the matter's all done and dusted.'

'You won't regret this, Mrs White. I'll be in touch,' the man said, almost bouncing out of the chair in his haste to leave. When he had gone, Mum sank back on her pillow like a deflated balloon.

'Who was that creep?' I asked.

'Mr Harris – I told you. Don't make a fuss, Lucy. You know it makes me tired.' Then she remembered something she disliked about our conversation, saying, 'What was it you said about that girl – Mariella? – I won't have her name mentioned in my hearing.'

'Why not?'

Mum considered for a bit. 'Because what's her name? Mariella and her... her *despicable* mother were responsible for making me ill. And when your Dad comes back, I'll tell him so. He's not going to get away with it, not this time.' She was off again.

'Dad's not coming back, Mum, you know that.' I put her things into the locker and kissed her. Just as I was leaving, she had another memory flash, as unexpected as ever.

'What happened to the silver fish?' she asked. 'You must

keep it safe until you need it.

'That's what Rhiannon said.'

'Rhiannon? You know her?' I had no intention of being drawn into answering difficult questions at this time of night, so I busied myself putting the washing in a plastic bag and mumbled something non-committal. But Mum wasn't listening anyway. 'Yes, Rhiannon was always worrying about things like that,' she mused. Then, sharply, 'You'll be back again tomorrow?'

'After school, Mum. I promise.'

'How was she?' Nan asked as we made for the bus stop.

'Exhausting,' I said. 'She's like a firecracker, forever leaping from one thing- one mood – to another. It's hard to keep track.' Something made me keep her creepy visitor to myself.

'Never mind, love. We'll have something quick to eat and an early night, just the two of us. It will all seem different in the morning.' Nan's judgement was right, as usual.

*

All that week Millie smirked and preened, smiling secret smiles and sighing. She looked very pleased with herself – a cat with a saucer of cream had nothing on her – but I couldn't rouse myself to comment. Henry seemed so last-weekend to me.

The daughters of Awar and their strange rituals gradually took on the fabric of a dream. I stowed the silver fish and its evil vibes at the bottom of my dressing table drawer, not caring if it ever saw the light of day again.

I stuck to my routine, visiting Mum every afternoon.

Sometimes she was with it, sometimes not. Sometimes Dad got it in the neck, at other times it was me. Mostly, not always, she was in denial about his death. Every day it grew more difficult to know where she was in her mind and to follow her Jack-in-the-box jumps. Nan's house was a haven – mostly, that is.

One evening, quite late, just as we were getting ready for bed, the bell rang and rang. It sounded urgent.

'OK, I'm coming,' Nan grumbled, unbolting the door. I was right behind her. A visitor at this time of night was a rarity.

Mariella. She was in shock, white-faced and gasping for breath, her hair standing up in spikes. 'I'm sorry, I'm sorry…' she said over and over again. 'A prowler – in the house – throwing things – chased me…'

'Calm down, my dear.' Nan was at her best. 'Come inside and tell us about it. You can't stand out here all night.' She drew the distressed girl into the hall. Under the light, Nan held her at arm's length and looked her up and down. 'Aren't you…?'

'Mariella,' I finished for her.

'I wanted to come and see you long before this, I really did, but I didn't dare,' Mariella said, standing awkwardly beside Nan.

'Don't worry about that now. What's this about a prowler? Have you managed to let the police know? No?' Nan was on the case, telephone in hand.

The police took Mariella very seriously, made notes, whispered into their shoulder microphones and tried to keep everyone calm. 'You're in charge of this young lady, I take it, Mrs White?' Mariella gazed at Nan with eyes like small moons and nodded slightly. Nan got the message.

'Yes, I am her grandmother,' she said – with complete truth.

You have to hand it to Nan. No one would have guessed she hadn't seen or heard of Mariella for years. Nor that she hadn't known that she was staying more or less around the corner.

When we trooped around to Mariella's house, we found that it had been comprehensively trashed. 'Anything missing?' a policewoman asked Nan.

Nan looked to Mariella for help. She shook her head, thought better of it, then said in a small voice, 'Yes, as a matter of fact, there is. My mother's favourite painting has gone – it's valuable, I think.'

'Nothing else?'

Nan looked to Mariella for confirmation. 'Not that we know of,' she said.

'What does this painting look like, miss?'

Mariella described my dad's painting in great detail. 'But I saw that picture over a week ago…' I couldn't help interrupting. I explained about the man who had visited Mum in the hospital, although I kept quiet about the document she'd signed.

'You're sure?'

'Sure,' I said.

We stood in the wrecked kitchen, but the other rooms

were in the same state. The contents of every drawer and cupboard had been tipped out onto the floor.

'Let me get this right,' the policeman said, 'This can't have been the first break-in then? Do you have more work by this artist, what was his name, Charles White?'

'No,' Mariella said, ''That's the only one my mother owns... she'll be in a terrible state when she finds out.' We were getting into deep water, the three of us, so Nan put an end to the questions by saying it was time she got us home.

Just before he reluctantly snapped his notebook shut, the policeman asked, 'And this young lady's mother, she is ... where?'

'In Scotland,' Mariella said quickly.

'Yes, my grand-daughter's with me for the moment,' Nan put in.

Once the police had gone, Nan said, 'You can't stay here on your own,' and she helped Mariella pack a bag with the bits and pieces she'd need to tide her over the next few days. After all, the two of them had a lot of catching up to do.

*

As we walked back, I reflected how strange it was that Dad's work seemed quite suddenly to have become the flavour of the month, and I was glad that I hadn't said anything about the pictures stacked at home in the loft. I must get hold of Henry, I thought, remembering that he'd offered to help. I wasn't ready for Nan, Mariella and the entire police force of South Wales to come crawling over our house, well, not until I'd done my own detective work.

That night Mariella was installed in a put-u-up bed squashed alongside mine and I had swiftly to learn the art of sharing with someone I'd only just met. It wasn't only my bedroom, of course. Worst of all, I had to share Nan. That wasn't going to be easy.

I fell into a troubled sleep. I saw myself walking right into the Llyncelyn picture, image and reality merging the way they do in dreams. I knew I was looking for something, something important, but what it was, I couldn't remember.

'Mariella?' I whispered. A snuffling response.

'What?'

'When did you last see my Dad's painting, the one you showed me?'

'Dunno. I don't look at it every day.'

'You've no idea when it went missing?'

She said she didn't and turned on her side, conversation over.

I resolved to get back to our house pronto, before the loathsome Harris had the same idea. As soon as it seemed civilised, I was up and ready to go. School would have to take a back seat today, I decided. Nan had to escort Mariella to the police station to sign statements and things, so I reckoned she would not be too bothered about what I was doing with myself.

'Bye,' I said to both of them, pecking Nan on the cheek

as I picked up my bag. 'Hope it goes well.' Then I zipped out of the door and ran to the bus stop. But I didn't get on the school bus.

'I need a few things from the shop,' I told a bewildered Millie. 'I'll catch up with you later.' Until now, I've never been one for bunking off, so I'm not altogether *au fait* with the safest way of going about it. But needs must. It seemed to work, mainly because nobody expected me to do it, I suppose. Anyway, I had more pressing things on my mind and phoned Henry.

'Are you still up for a tour round my dad's paintings? I asked.

'Sure,' he said, his voice slurred with sleep. 'What time?'

We arranged to meet at the back of the house in half an hour. Less conspicuous than hanging around the front door, I thought.

'Don't try to go in on your own,' he warned.

CHAPTER EIGHT

Just as well, as it happened.

I lingered in a back garden that had become almost unrecognisable. The lawn was a tall wilderness, starred with dandelions and spindly buttercups. Only a few hardy roses and day-lilies bloomed above the rampant weeds which had crowned themselves kings of the border. Mum, who liked order in the garden, would have hated it, but it wouldn't have bothered Dad. He had always liked the lived-in look.

'Hi, Luce!' Henry strolled through the gate, a mere matter of ten minutes late. 'How are things?' He waved a copy of the *Western Times* in my direction. 'Seen this?'

'Lost modernist found' shouted a headline in the arts section. The article told how an outstanding painting had been rescued from a junk shop window. 'It is thought to be part of a collection destroyed by Charles White, the secretive local artist, before his tragic death last year.'

'Destroyed? Who says? Let me look.' I grabbed the paper from Henry. It went on to give a quote from his widow, interviewed in her hospital bed, 'My husband was suffering from severe depression… unhappy with the standard of his work' blah, blah.'

Henry was speed-reading over my shoulder. 'What a load of rubbish!'

'I told you Mum doesn't know what she's saying half the

time. She's the one with severe depression.'

'But how did they…?'

I filled Henry in about the Harris guy as we made our way round to the front door. I was as certain as I could be that he was making money out of this somewhere along the line.

'He got Mum to sign a document – and she's in no fit state. Then he was out of the door like a rat up a drainpipe.'

Standing in the sunshine on our front doorstep, I re-read the article more carefully, half of me thrilled to think that Dad's 'bold and vivid' work was finally getting the attention it deserved, the other half furious about the lies. Dad depressed? No way. How I wished he were still around, not only to enjoy his fame but to set the record straight.

'Is there a Charles White treasure trove still to be discovered?' the journalist asked his readers. The story was illustrated with a muzzy black and white photograph of the Llyncelyn seascape, last seen in the hands of Harris.

Henry stood, waiting for me to finish reading. 'Somebody's having problems,' he observed. Across the road, we heard a van starting up with a great deal of spluttering. Then it chugged off in a cloud of exhaust fumes.

I folded Henry's copy of the *Western Times,* returned it and fished out my key.

'You think that the Harris bloke is behind all this?' Henry asked. 'We'd better get our skates on and make sure the pictures are OK before we decide what to do next.'

Too late. Harris and his gang had been there before us.

'I reckon they're the characters in the clapped-out van. Probably going out the front door as we were coming round from the back.'

'Dad's paintings?' I squeaked. 'They're taking them away! Can't we stop them?'

'You can, if you like,' Henry said. 'I'm no hero!' Sensible, dependable Henry, just like Dad said. 'Let's check the damage.'

*

Although the house still had its sad peopleless smell, drawers sagged open and the mail was strewn across the hall floor. Obviously, people had come and gone. There was a dark patch on the sitting room wall where one of Dad's pictures used to hang.

We made our way cautiously through the downstairs rooms, finding a broken window in the larder.

'Just as well I was late,' Henry commented, 'otherwise we might have met the burglars face to face.'

We found the loft ladder pulled down. 'Attic first stop, I take it,' Henry said. As I watched his battered trainers disappearing into the loft space, I remembered Dad comparing him to a second-hand car and couldn't help smiling.

'What's the joke?' he asked as I heaved my way up behind him.

'Nothing. Just thinking about something Dad once said.' When our eyes got used to the dim light, we saw that the devastation wasn't as bad as we feared. 'They couldn't manage them all at once, I reckon.'

Stacked behind empty easels, standing legs akimbo, we found eight pictures left face to the wall. 'Will we get them all in your car?' I asked.

'I walked,' Henry said bleakly.

We sat among the tubes of hardening paint and stiffened brushes. 'It didn't take Harris long to suss out this hoard,' I said.

'We should get on to the police pronto,' Henry said, but it proved to be a long and tedious business. Nobody appeared to have heard of Charles White or his paintings. Nor did telling them of the write-up in the *Western Times* excite much interest.

'We'll send someone round as soon as we can,' they promised.

'That's a fat lot of good,' I complained. 'I bet Harris is gloating over the stuff in Bristol or somewhere by now.'

'If he hasn't sold it on,' said Henry gloomily. 'Not much joined-up writing there. You'd have thought they might have matched it up with Mariella's break-in.'

We turned the remaining paintings around and had a good look at them. I could almost feel dad's breath on the back of my neck.

'Strange,' Henry said, standing back and taking stock. 'They're all landscapes, no sign of a portrait anywhere. I thought your dad was big on that kind of thing. I imagined we'd find loads of nudes.'

'Not of Mum, that's for sure. According to Nan, she binned the lot.'

'Afraid she might cause a stir? Respected doctor's wife and all that?'

'Afraid that Rhiannon's lot would put a spell on her, more like,' I said, remembering how forbidding they'd sounded about 'the rules.'

Henry started to root about, anxious to make sure we hadn't missed anything. No joy. Then he cannoned into me, almost knocking me over. Or so I thought.

'Hey, watch it,' I said, arms flailing.

Henry looked offended. 'I don't know what you're on about. I haven't moved a centimetre.'

'OK, maybe I tripped.' Although I knew I hadn't.

I steadied myself on a dark narrow ledge tucked under the eaves where my outstretched fingers found a package not much bigger than a postcard. It was wrapped in stained paint rags.

Henry stood transfixed as I slowly unwrapped the parcel to reveal a tiny picture. It was delicate, a miniature, done in spidery brush strokes. On the back, in my father's writing, *The Dancing Daughter.* I swear I heard the echo of Dad's laughter.

The miniature was a finished version of the sketch I'd found of Mum dancing – naked. In it, she looked more beautiful than ever. What was it dad had said in his notes? - *sun-streaked?* – the little picture glowed with jewelled colour, the figure backlit in some halo effect and the ribbons were green of course.

'She must have been looking for this when she had her accident,' I said. 'She was desperate to get rid of something – what do you think this business of banning portraits is all about? Bad luck?'

'It's probably more to do with stealing the soul – some tribes won't be photographed because of it.'

'That figures,' I said, thinking back to the shenanigans that took place at Llyncelyn last weekend.

Henry took the picture over to the skylight to see it better. 'It's fantastic,' he said. 'You can see what the newspaper people were on about. You'd better take care of it.' I took the little portrait into safekeeping. Mine, I decided. A present from Dad to me, of that I was dead sure.

We crawled about among spider webs and assorted junk in an attempt to check that there was no more important stuff lurking about.

'Still seeing Millie?' I asked, hoping I'd not made it sound too important.

Henry hesitated. 'Sort of,' he finally admitted. 'She's getting a tad serious, crowding me, if you know what I mean, so I'm backing off a bit.' Silly-Millie, I thought to myself, but I was pleased in a mean kind of way.

*

It was Henry who first came across the yellowing newspaper. It was streaked with paint as though Dad had been trying out colours. That made it difficult to read, but we managed to make out the headline, *'LOCAL DOCTOR'S WIFE MISSING.'* A fading Botticelli-beautiful picture of my mother accompanied a short article about her mysterious disappearance.

'She's got clothes on this time,' Henry said, sounding disappointed. 'But she's still some looker, your mum,' – this with genuine admiration. Then, noting the date – late July the year before I was born – he added matter-of-factly, 'I reckon that's when you came into the picture.'

I gazed from the miniature to the brittle photograph of this young woman, my mother, looking as far away as a fairy tale, but there wasn't time to do more than skim through the old newspaper story. I really wanted to study it in private – not here, not now, among the debris of redundant brushes and dried-out paints and the growing possibility that my father wasn't my father after all. I sank into the dust of the attic, tears spilling down my cheeks.

Henry knelt beside me. 'Luce,' he said, 'Luce, I wish I could do something,' patting me big-brother like, on the shoulder.

'You can't, Henry. Nobody can. I don't even know who I am. Lucy White or Lucy Someone Else?' I was gulping with tears by this time.

'But, Lucy, you're still you. No different to the girl you were last week, last month, last year, I promise you.' Henry was baffled, not sure how to deal with me. His eyes grew huge and solemn and his glasses gleamed in the dim light.

I sat there, rocking and juddering, crushing the scrap of old newspaper in my hand, unable to get one sensible word out.

All I wanted at that minute was to be safe at home with my Nan, not Mariella's. How I hated that thought.

Up till now, I'd been so busy trying to put the jigsaw pieces of my life together that I'd almost banished the feeling of not belonging. I thought back to how safe I'd felt until Mum dropped her bombshell. Before that, I had never given my identity a second thought. Lucy White, the doctor's daughter.

'It's not only Dad,' I gulped. 'There's Mum and…' I couldn't go on.

'And that batty lot at Llyncelyn,' Henry finished for me. 'Well, you had to go to pieces sometime. You've coped brilliantly – especially with your mum so ill and all…'

I swallowed hard. 'We'd better get on,' I said, sniffing. 'We've got masses to do before the police arrive.' And, of course, I'd skipped school and didn't intend to do it again. I'd better make today's foray worthwhile, I thought.

'That's more like it,' Henry said. He sounded relieved and tried to mop my tears with balled-up tissues. Unfortunately, he'd picked them up from the floor, so they covered my face with dust and made me sneeze. He sat back on his heels and looked at me critically, no doubt comparing me to the picture of my mother. *'You're* certainly no oil painting at this moment,' he said.

I scrunched the newspaper into my pocket and got myself together. I put the dancing portrait safely into my bag before we began to struggle downstairs with the left-over canvases, commenting now and then on Dad's use of colour and the way he'd brought landscapes to life with a few strokes of his brush. No wonder the art world was so keen.

'Fantastic,' Henry breathed as he stood upright. I beamed with pride. This was my dad he was talking about and, judging by today's papers, lots of other people were keen to get in on the act.

'D'you think we've got everything?' We had assembled all eight Charles Whites in the upstairs hall.

When a couple of bored policemen finally appeared, they took notes, looked at the broken window and said they'd send a fingerprint expert when they had someone available. Stolen paintings didn't seem high on their list of priorities.

'Ready to go and get the car?' I asked. 'We'd better hide the pictures before we leave, just in case...'

'In case Harris and his gang come back? I suppose you're right.'

We gave every hiding place in the house the once-over, but none of them was right. Henry voted for the bathroom. 'They'll never think of looking for a picture in there. Drape some towels over them.

'What if they need the loo? How about under the bed?'

'Too obvious.'

We agreed eventually to stash them at the back of the wardrobe and to cover them over with Mum's drab dresses. Not brilliant, but the best we could do. The wardrobe's selling point was its key. I locked it and dropped the key into the pocket of my jeans.

The house seemed so cold and alien that I couldn't wait to leave. 'It's like being in a black-and-white version of a place I once knew,' I said, trying to explain to Henry how weird I found it. 'Have I turned into a ghost, do you think?'

'A pretty substantial ghost,' Henry commented. 'Anything else you need to pick up? Letters? Certificates? There must be some kind of an answer to the questions bugging you.' I shook my head.

'So that's it then?' Henry still sounded reluctant. 'I'm sure there's something more if only we could crack it,' he said, carefully closing all the doors leading into the hall.

The door to the understairs cupboard wouldn't shut properly. 'There's something stopping it,' Henry said. 'You've looked in here, I take it?'

How could I have forgotten? 'There's an army of black bags full of stuff for charity in there. Millie and I didn't have time to look through them last time.'

'What are we waiting for?' Henry was tireless. 'Let's stack them in the hall and tackle them one by one. Somewhere there's one essential clue we've missed, there must be!' Not only tireless but methodical, our Henry.

We lugged the bags, five of them, into the hall and lined them against the wall.

'Remind me never to volunteer for Oxfam,' I said, having dragged the depressing contents of the first one onto the floor. Mostly Dad's clothes, old shirts, pants, socks. Nothing exciting.

Henry's luck was no better. He had a load of paperbacks, war stories, back copies of *Artist's World,* that kind of thing. He paused, magazine in the air. 'Listen,' he whispered.

From the kitchen came the sound of voices. We should have made our escape while the going was good.

CHAPTER NINE

'About my dad?' I said.

'*Our* dad.' Mariella gazed across the table at me. Her eyes were serious, grey like Dad's. We had made it to the Costa Coffee place in town in a Nan-inspired attempt to do the sister-cum-friend bit.

I swallowed, accepting the inevitable. 'Did you see him a lot, our dad, I mean? At your house? When?' The questions tumbled out. Maybe I wasn't even sure I wanted answers.

Mariella thought for a long moment. 'Well, I first remember him as a soft-spoken man coming to see us from time to time when I was little. He always wanted to give me a hug, play with me, that kind of thing. I must have been a complete pain because I wouldn't have anything to do with him. He wasn't a total stranger, of course, but I was a bit frightened of him…'

Frightened of Dad? 'He was the gentlest man in the world,' I said.

'Yes, but I wasn't used to a man about the place. And sometimes he made my mother cry.'

'Why? I thought he loved her?'

'Perhaps that was the problem.' Mariella looked puzzled. 'Although he desperately wanted to, he couldn't stay. It upset Mum, upset me, come to that. Anyway we solved it by disappearing to Scotland – I went to school there – so I didn't see him for years.'

'Did you know about him? Know who you were, I mean?'

'Obviously, I knew I had a father – knew too, that he had an *official* family. So, for me, you've always been around, but invisible. Mum and I were a complete unit, so I wasn't particularly curious about him. All I knew was that he was a doctor who lived in Wales. To be honest, he was out of sight, out of mind. I hardly gave him a thought.'

'So you didn't keep in touch?'

'Not that I know of, well, not until I took ill a couple of years ago. But I'm OK now,' she said hurriedly. 'Mum was worried that it might be a hereditary thing, so naturally Charles got involved. To make it easier, we rented a place close by and he organised lots of scans and blood tests for me, the complete works. So he came back into our lives in a big way.'

Our coffee had gone cold. I was beginning to feel almost sorry for this half-sister of mine when I remembered – what was it Mum had said? *'He wasn't your real father, you know.'* At least Mariella was sure of hers.

'As I began to get better, I wanted to see what you looked like, so I spied on you from time to time. I watched you getting off the school bus, giggling with your friends, getting into the car with Charles. Funny, I didn't often see you with your mum – although I know you did the family outing bit occasionally.' This with a shadow of envy in her voice.

The idea of a stalker hiding behind the hedge for months made my skin crawl. It was like being seen from the inside of a

TV set, like a *Big Sister watching!* How much of my private life had she viewed?

'I stopped doing it after he died.' She paused to see how I was taking it.

'Why?'

'It didn't seem fair.' Our conversation stalled.

I needed to move away from her cool, almost spiteful, stare. She seemed so much older, so much more self-possessed than me. I ordered another mocha for Mariella, a skinny latte for myself, before changing tack.

'How did you meet Henry?'

'You know my mum's a sculptor…?'

I nodded.

'And Henry's doing a degree in geology?' I'd forgotten.

'So?'

'Mum was doing research into local stone when she discovered Henry. His dissertation specialises in the rocks and stones of South Wales, so his tutor suggested they meet. He visited her in her studio and they got talking. She was sorry for him, living alone and all that, so she invited him back for a meal and the rest they say…'

'Is history,' I finished. 'Henry does the little-boy-lost beautifully. Nan feels the same way about him. It must be the short-sighted eyes and the Harry Potter glasses that have that effect.'

'That look doesn't work so well for females,' Mariella

commented.

'I'd noticed.' Sharing the first shard of girly togetherness, we exchanged a wry smile.

Mariella licked the last of the cream from her spoon. 'Time to get on, d'you think?'

We strolled among the summer crowds and stood for a moment watching a pavement artist recreate famous paintings on the piazza floor. He used a range of coloured chalks and worked in fast confident strokes. I was fascinated by his skill and dropped some change into his hat.

'Loser,' Mariella said curtly. She was more interested in the fashionable shop windows and impatient to move on.

We're never going to be bosom pals, I thought. My half-sister was too cynical, too cruel. I took stock of her when she wasn't looking, trying to find echoes of Dad in her. Was it in her deep laugh? the wide grey eyes? the raised eyebrow?

'Do you do any painting or drawing?' I asked.

'Not me, I leave all that stuff to my mum. I draw the way a cobra flies!'

Although I had decided to hate Mariella's mother more than anyone else in the world – well, who wouldn't? she'd stolen my dad, after all, - I surprised myself by saying, 'I'd like to see your Mum's work sometime.' All in the spirit of research, I silently assured myself.

The opportunity was to come sooner than we thought.

*

Nan was entertaining a visitor in the kitchen by the time we got back. She was the last person I either expected or wanted to meet that afternoon.

Nan introduced us. 'Meet Arabella, Mariella's mum. This is Lucy, my other granddaughter.' *Other!* I stood rooted by the table, smouldering with rage. How could Nan, of all people, let me down like this? More to give myself something to do than anything else, I moved to the fridge and poured a drink. 'Anyone else?' I asked vaguely, rudely too, no doubt.

'Sit down, Lucy. You're making me dizzy wandering around like that.' Nan could be a proper grandmother when she put her mind to it. I did as I was told, glowering at the visitor from under my fringe.

She was plump as a pigeon (Mariella had inherited her mother's figure, I decided, meanly) with a halo of wispy grey hair. Her face was striking but no longer young-looking and creased with worry lines like spider webs. She wore dangly silver earrings and rattling bangles and was hung about with a long velvet scarf in rainbow colours. Her hands, out of kilter with the rest of her, were workmanlike with thick fingers and short-trimmed nails, innocent of nail varnish. In fact, they were none too clean by the looks of them.

I glared at Mariella's mother, a bad taste rising in my throat. I hated her and blamed her for being the last person in the world to have spoken to my dad. I could no more drink my Coke than fly.

Uncharacteristically silent, I tried to figure out what was so special about this woman, what had propelled my dad towards her. She was no great beauty, but I had to admit, she was an interesting-looking person, as unlike Mum as you could find anywhere. She had caused Dad's death – hadn't she called him out? – and I couldn't forgive her. And yet I wanted, needed, to find out more about her.

'What's all this about Charles's picture?' I heard her ask.

Senses on the alert, I tumbled back into the conversation. 'A break-in, I take it?'

Mariella put her glass on the table with such care that it might have been made of crystal. 'Grandma White told you our house had been burgled?' And ours, I thought.

'I shouldn't have left you all this time on your own. But I've been so wretched since Charles died. I didn't mean to be away so long... you weren't hurt, sweetheart?'

'No, I ran for my life when I heard them.' She twiddled the glass, looking away from the rest of us. 'They made an awful mess, but they didn't actually take anything.'

'What about...?'

Mariella had a confession to make. I could see her winding herself up. 'I've done something terrible, Mum.' She ran her finger round the rim of the glass. 'It wasn't them. It was me. *I* took the picture Charles gave you to the antique, well, to the junk shop on the corner.'

Granny's Goodies, I knew it well. (Mariella didn't call

my dad, *Dad,* I noted and was secretly pleased.)

'You *what?'* Arabella sounded none too forgiving.

'Mum, I'm so sorry,' she went on in a small voice. 'You see, I'd run out of money and it was the only thing I could think of… After all, it was only a picture, not rings or anything like that.'

'So, it wasn't stolen?' Nan looked bemused.

'No.' We were all stunned. Mariella's face had gone white.

'Why has Dad become famous all of a sudden?' I asked, startling everyone, including myself, by suddenly finding my voice. I produced the *Western Times* article from the depths of my bag and flattened it out on the table top. 'Is it because he's dead?'

'Well, that too probably,' Arabella said, scrabbling for her glasses. 'You see, he had a big exhibition half-promised for the autumn. Cardiff first, then we were hoping for a London venue. Pie in the sky, I'm afraid. After his wonderful *The Dancing Daughter* was rejected for the Royal Academy summer show last year, he became ultra-superstitious and didn't say a word about it to anyone.'

I felt for a moment like Dad's ghost had kicked me, although I wasn't about to let on that that very picture was hiding under my pillow. 'He said nothing, even to me.'

'No, well, he wouldn't. He didn't dare let Grace find out. He thought she'd be sure to put a spanner in the works.'

I suppose he had a point. Mum would have thrown a

major wobbly, no doubt about it. Anything remotely related to his painting sparked off the sudden need to be looked after hand, foot and finger 24/7.

'That's one reason why Charles came over on Christmas Eve. His exhibition had just been given the green light and we wanted to celebrate. And, of course, there were the presents...'

'So that's why you opened the champagne! You might have told me,' Mariella chipped in.

'We were under strict instructions to say nothing, not a cheep, until the press release. But now? I wonder who's behind this?' She picked up the newspaper cutting, read it carefully and passed it to Nan.

'Somebody somewhere knows that Charles White was not simply any old GP,' Nan said.

I took a deep breath and, like Mariella, told them all that had happened: Harris, bunking off, the break-in, everything.

It was mind-boggling to realise that, instead of screaming accusations, I was calmly explaining things to Dad's... I couldn't think quite how to put it... other half, lover, mistress? Arabella, mother of Dad's other daughter. At the back of my mind, I felt as though *I,* not Dad this time, was in some way being unfaithful to my mother. But it was only a tiny twinge of conscience. Truth to tell, I was fascinated by Arabella too. Like father, like daughter?

'Harris, did you say? What does he look like?' Arabella asked. I tried to describe him – then I had a better idea. I got hold of Nan's telephone pad and scribbled what I could remember of the narrow head, sparse hair, mean close-together eyes, the little moustache. 'Not perfect, but not too far off,' I said.

Arabella studied it. 'Not Harris, Hartog I bet – a notorious dealer. Never known to pay anything like the full price. How much did your mum sign it away for? D'you know?'

'No idea,' I said. 'I was only too glad to see the back of him.'

'Well, as it was a present from Charles to me many moons ago, I'm going to make it my business to follow it up.' Arabella sounded very determined. Harris doesn't stand a chance with her on the case, I thought. And, being in the art world herself, she was no doubt pretty knowledgeable.

After Mariella and her mother had left for their flat, Nan waded in, 'Not very bright, Lucy-girl. I thought Henry had more sense. Anything could have happened to you…'

'But it didn't.'

'True,' she said, and the telling-off was over.

As we sat over supper, she confided, 'I never expected to meet her again, you know. We'd promised your mother, your Dad and me, way back, when you were born.'

'He didn't keep his promise, Nan,' I said.

'To be fair, he kept his side of the bargain for years, didn't see them – well, not until they came back here – no more than a couple of years ago, I'd say.'

Arabella had a different take on the story.

CHAPTER TEN

Millie called. 'I saw a lot of stuff about your dad in the papers. How about a night on the town, and you can bring me up to speed?' Millie is always desperate to be in the thick of things – she doesn't take kindly to being kept on the outside. 'Surely you're due a night off from your sick visiting?'

'What about Henry? Doesn't he have first call on your Saturday nights?'

'It does no harm to make them sweat,' Millie said. She could be incredibly callous at times. So – maybe she wasn't all that interested in Henry anyway.

'It might be a good idea to make it a threesome,' Nan suggested. 'Take Mariella with you. She deserves some fun.'

'Do I have to?'

'No, you don't 'have to', but I think you should.'

I didn't put up a fight.

Millie was fascinated by the lost-sister-found-sister story. She and Mariella seemed to hit it off immediately, bosom buddies five minutes after first meeting. Amazing. I began to feel like the odd one out.

What is it about me? I wondered. Am I some sort of matchmaker? Has the Llyncelyn spell rubbed off on me?

'How does it feel to have a famous father?' Millie asked. Mariella and I looked at one another, for the first time, unsure of who should answer.

'Strange,' we said, more or less together.

'But I'd like it a lot more if he was here to enjoy it,' I said. Millie had the grace to look a bit embarrassed.

'Me too,' said Mariella – a touch of sisterly solidarity? Like it or not, I was going to have to get used to sharing my dad.

We took the bus into town. It was gearing up to be the usual happy-go-lucky Saturday night and I wasn't sure I was ready to cope with it. Girls like ourselves were going about in gangs, arms linked, giggling and showing off, especially when teenage lads hove into sight. There was a lot of bare flesh on view and I began to feel distinctly over-dressed.

We strolled down the main street, casting our eyes over shop windows where the clothes on display, although elegant, looked out of the ark. It was good to be away from the black dog that had been riding on my shoulder for so long and to realise that there is still a big wide world out there.

We paused outside a late-opening music shop, debating where to go next. Millie gazed into the black hole of the next-door trendy pub. 'They've got a fabulous happy hour in here,' she said. 'Shall we?'

There was no stopping them. Dressed to the nines, Millie and Mariella could easily be taken for eighteen, I suppose. Mariella was obviously delighted to be part of the scene. She and Millie were getting on like a house on fire. More like sisters than the real thing!

'Catch you up later,' I said. The music shop was more my

bag. I selected a couple of tracks and put the headphones on. There must have been some mistake. Instead of Cerys Matthews, I was treated to reedy nose-flute music. The hairs on the back of my neck trembled. The Daughters of Awar hadn't finished with me. I felt propelled into action.

Almost breathless, I caught up with the others. 'I've got to get to the hospital,' I told them. 'I must see my mum before it's too late.'

'What now?' Millie said. 'Did your nan call you?

'No... yes.' It was too difficult to explain. I knew somehow that I didn't have much time.

I puffed into the ward just as the bell rang for the end of visiting hour. 'Good, you made it. Your mother has been asking for you,' the charge nurse told me. 'She's been pretty restless.'

Not now, she wasn't. She was lying unmoving against the pillows, a bright scarlet spot on each cheek, oxygen mask over her mouth. She pulled the mask away to greet me.

'Lucy,' she said. 'I knew you'd come.' Great, she knows me, I thought. 'Got a kiss for your mummy?' I hadn't called her mummy for years, not since she stopped dressing in flounces and doing her little girl act. She grabbed my hand and held it tight.

'Is Dad home?' she asked.

'Not at the moment.' This was true.

'I want him to do something for me, something important.'

'What's that?'

'I need my green gown. Will you tell him, please Lucy?' Had the Daughters of Awar been whispering in her ears as well? I wondered.

She struggled to sit up. Then, out of the blue, she said, 'I saw the white raven last night.' Despite the late-evening warmth, shivers snaked down my spine. 'It's a sign.'

'Of what?' but, of course, I knew the answer. And I was very frightened.

'It's an old Welsh legend – a story my mothers told me.'

'Your *mothers?*'

'Everyone has a mother, stands to reason,' she said. 'But I was special – I had lots of mothers. Did I never tell you?' She groped for the mask and sucked in air. I murmured something and kept quiet, not wanting to break the spell. Mum closed her eyes. Don't clam up on me now, please don't. I waited. Nothing.

'The white raven?' I prompted.

Her eyes lit up and she pulled the mask away. *'When a mother dies, the white raven flies,'* she chanted in a sing-song voice. 'I'm a mother, so it must be meant for me.'

'Mum, Mum, please don't die!' I pleaded, beside myself by this time. I kept hold of her hand, bony as any skeleton's nowadays. 'If you do, I'll have nobody.'

'I was fit in those days, very fit. Of course, I danced a lot. And sometimes I went swimming. It depended on which mother I was with at the time. Alwyn was my favourite – lovely and cuddly, she was. She used to sing me to sleep at night.' She went quiet for a minute, remembering, while I tried to grapple with the idea of having a different mother for different things.

'Alwyn taught me to read too, I remember.'

'Didn't you go to school?'

'The Daughters didn't believe in schools. The Daughters taught me everything I needed to know – the names of wildflowers, where birds like to nest, old songs and legends... lots of things... how to make Welsh cakes...' Her voice tailed off to a whisper.

She had passed none of this knowledge on to me. 'You've never said anything about when you were little, Mum. And I've never seen a photograph; I've often wondered about that.'

'The daughters didn't do photographs – or portraits, come to that – took some of their power away, they said.' She sighed. 'I've done my best to forget all those years. The white raven brought it back, Llyncelyn, the mothers.' Then, in a whisper, 'Remember Charles? He saved me, brought me to the big city.' She looked at me closely. 'Of course you remember him. He was your...' Now we're getting somewhere, '... your doctor.'

'My *father,*' I said.

'He might have been, yes.' She tightened her grip. 'I'm not a bad mother, Lucy, am I?'

''course not,' I whispered.

'All I ever wanted, you see, was to have a proper family with one mother and one father in a proper house with a garden and a room of my own, to know who I really was.'

Me too, I thought. 'But you were Grace Williams,' I said, 'so there must have been a Mrs – or maybe a Miss Williams somewhere…'

A thin cynical laugh. 'They said my real mother called me Grace, but the Williams bit came from the telephone directory. It was a very common name. They thought it would do.' Silence. 'They never found her, you know.'

I wasn't so sure. I'd bet anything she's one of those green-clad women at *Badpenny House,* I thought.

The charge nurse looked round the door. 'Everything OK?' he asked brightly.

Mum immediately snapped back into a passable imitation of her old self. 'Yes thanks,' she said. 'My daughter's just leaving.' And, in a fierce whisper, 'Don't forget to ask Dad for my green gown. It's in the top drawer of my dressing table.'

I tried to get myself together. 'Don't worry, Mum. I'll bring it,' I promised. 'Anything else?'

I really fancy a honey yoghurt, she said dreamily. 'I haven't had one of those in years. It used to be my favourite breakfast, do you remember, Lucy?' Her mind was still skipping like a stone across water.

I kissed her. 'Wear the silver fish,' she hissed after me. 'Just in case…'

Mum died that night. So she didn't have the honey yoghurt, but she did get to wear the green gown – for her funeral. And, at my throat, I wore the silver fish.

'Parcel for you, Lucy,' Nan said. It was from Rhiannon – how she tracked down Nan's address, I'll never know.

I tore it open. Inside a bulky envelope and a note.

'We were so sorry to hear of your loss,' the note said. 'Your mother, our daughter.' On the back, a scrawled PS, 'Remember to wear your silver fish.' I traced its slim shape with my fingers. I was becoming used to wearing it now.

In the envelope, I found a pair of tiny scuffed ballet shoes that had once been green, a book of Welsh legends and a label with the single word, **GRACE** on it, lettered carefully in Italic script.

'Let's see.' Nan could hardly contain her curiosity. 'Someone must have treasured this,' she said of the label. 'It looks as though it had been done yesterday.'

The little shoes were a shock, small enough to hold in the palm of my hand. More tangible than any photograph, they brought my mother's babyhood into sudden focus. I imagined the small red-haired child trying them on, one of her mothers doing up the ribbons, giving her a kiss. Was she proud? excited? impatient to show off her new shoes? Had she danced in the dark back room of *Badpenny House* or outside in the garden? I was loath to put them down.

The book of legends was another matter. I riffled through it, all dense text, no illustrations, although each story was framed by an intricate black and white border. It would need my concentrated attention sometime, not now. Too detailed, too difficult. Henry, I thought. He's the one person who would understand their significance. I couldn't wait to tell him.

'A memory box,' Nan was saying. 'That's what you need for all the stuff about your mum.'

Good idea, I suppose. Other people have photograph albums, I have a memory box.

I didn't know how I should reply to Rhiannon. I felt no sense of connection to her. 'Just say thank you and let it go at that,' Nan said. 'Do it now and get it out of the way.'

Good advice. Writing the address on the envelope brought the whole Llyncelyn experience back. I shuddered, pushing it away. When the card dropped into the post box, I promised myself never to think about Llyncelyn again – ever. It's the future for me now, 'onwards and upwards' as Dad used to say, especially as I have the Charles White retrospective to look forward to.

*

Arabella had got her teeth firmly into the business of the dreaded Harris character. She had listened patiently to my version of events, nodding now and again.

'It's got Hartog's fingerprints all over it,' she'd said.

*

When Henry and I first heard the footsteps, I had been too terrified to scream. Henry shoved me, bag and all, head-first into the understairs cupboard and pulled the door closed behind us.

Slow hesitant footsteps. A mumbled 'Bloody hell!' as blokes stumbled into the pile of black bags.

'Someone's beaten us to it,' one said. 'Better check there's nobody about.' We heard doors being opened and closed. 'The birds have flown,' they agreed.

They tipped the contents of the black bags on the floor. 'Nothing worthwhile. Just old clothes and books. Not even a boot sale would take this junk.'

Then a voice right beside us. 'Possibly not his best, but take it anyway. The name alone will sell it the way things are going at the moment.'

We'd forgotten a small painting hanging by the front door.

'We'd better get cracking upstairs. The boss'll kill us if the rest of the stuff's gone.'

They kept up a whispered conversation, more like a kind of impatient shorthand with a good bit of swearing thrown in. Then, footsteps on the metal steps of the loft ladder, a frustrated yell, 'Told you! Some bugger's been here!'

We took a chance and heaved at the cupboard door, trying desperately to keep the noise down. But our exit was blocked. 'These bloody bags,' Henry hissed. 'They'll hear us a mile off.'

Sure enough. 'Thought you said this so-and-so place was empty,' a voice complained. 'I'm convinced I heard something.'

'Too much beer, that's your trouble – unless, of course, you think it's haunted.' Laughter. 'C'mon. We'd better shift ourselves out of here. The boss'll go bananas!'

Saved by the bell, the front doorbell, that is. A couple of polite ding-dongs, then a rattling of the letterbox.

'This should be fun,' Henry whispered.

'Police! Open up!' The intruders had left the back door unlocked for a quick getaway – and an easy way-in for the police.

The Harris Two were well and truly trapped. We heard a great commotion as they were grabbed and led away.

We felt more than a little foolish, banging on the cupboard door to be let out. 'A new take on an old joke,' one of the young policemen said, as he released us.

We dusted ourselves down. 'That was a bit of luck,' said one of the team.

'And to think we only came along to take fingerprints.'

They were on a high.

We showed them where we had hidden the paintings and were whisked off to 'help in their enquiries.' It was like being in a film. Exciting at first, then boring as there was a lot of waiting around.

As we sat drinking our third coffee, I took the opportunity. 'Henry,' I said, 'Tell me about Mariella. How did you meet her?' Anything to keep my mind off Dad's missing paintings.

'Through Arabella.' He told me about the sculpture studio, but I headed him off before the lecture on the kinds of stone indigenous to South Wales. 'I must say, I find the whole sculpture thing fascinating,' he finished.

I was interested, in spite of myself.

'I met your dad at Arabella's place, you know.'

'Often?' I asked.

'Once or twice. And he was definitely the man of the house, not just a visitor– or a doctor on a house visit.'

'How could you tell?'

'Partly it was the easy way they all talked and…'

'And?'

'Partly the way he looked at Arabella. His eyes kind of lit up. I'd never seen your dad look like that before.' Henry paused to see how I was taking it. 'And, of course, he knew where to put his hands on tea bags, light bulbs, a screwdriver – things like that.'

I felt so jealous my throat nearly closed up.

'Could you come through, please?' we were asked. 'A few more details and we're done.'

*

'That was it?' Arabella had been taking notes while I'd been talking. I didn't, of course, tell her everything, just the Hartog – or Harris – story. 'Hartog himself didn't turn up?'

I don't know how Arabella did it. She must have moved mountains, but before long, the paintings, all of them, were back in safe-keeping. Not only that, she had organised an exhibition of his work in one of the most prestigious galleries in town. The papers were full of it.

CHAPTER ELEVEN

'You're so like your dad,' Arabella said. 'Same nose, same grey eyes – and the same talent, by the looks of it. It's almost like having a bit of Charles back again.'

'But you've got Mariella.'

'Who's more like me than her father.'

I was warming to Arabella. She had invited me out for pasta, just the two of us – a kind of bonding thing. Or perhaps just a way of getting to know one another. We were having lunch in the Italian place where I had first unloaded Mum's bombshell onto Henry at the beginning of the long summer.

'Are you 100% sure I'm my dad's daughter?' I asked Arabella now.

'Of course you are.' She leaned across the table and hugged me. 'What put that funny idea in your head?'

'It was something Mum hinted at.'

'Well, forget it. She didn't always get things right.' Arabella's expression was serious. 'It's hard for me to talk about her, but she's had problems for years, problems in her mind - you know about that, of course?'

Tell me about it, I thought. Aloud I said, 'I know she suffered from depression.' I still felt very defensive about her.

'It was more than that – she had schizophrenia.' This was the first time anyone had spelt it out in cold blood. Even Dad hadn't given her 'problems' a name. 'That's why she had all those mood swings,' Arabella said. 'It was something to do with her upbringing, I guess. The medics say it's a way of coping with intolerable childhood stress.'

My poor mother, I thought. Everyone, including me, just assumed she was a bit batty.

The waitress brought drinks and took our order. It was such a fantastic menu that I found it difficult to make up my mind. Arabella chose ricotta and herb cannelloni. I settled for spaghetti with tomato and garlic sauce.

While we waited, I fiddled with my glass, not quite meeting Arabella's eyes. 'How did you and Dad meet?' – I *had* to ask.

'On a painting holiday in Devon. I was a tutor and your dad was a so-called student – but with such talent!'

'And you hit it off?'

'The old cliché – love at first sight. But he was married, off-limits – or so I believed.' Arabella twirled a silver ring, third finger, *right* hand, I noted. 'We really did try to keep things secret – especially as your mother was so vulnerable…'

I could imagine her, the fragile girl-wife in gauzy skirts, on her own at home, trusting him, playing out her fairytale.

'Of course, she eventually found out - and by that time I was expecting. Not surprisingly, I suppose, she went completely off the rails and disappeared. It was all over the papers.' She sighed. 'She went off to join some cult – spooked your father, it did, when he managed to track her down.' A pause. 'I promised never to contact him again.' I thought of the paint-spattered cutting, *LOCAL DOCTOR'S WIFE MISSING.*

'So?'

'So I never did. Well, not intentionally.'

I carried the image of 'Mariella, three months' in my head. I dug out the photograph.

'Yes, well – he wanted to see his baby daughter, to hold her just once, to show her off to her grandmother. But Mariella and I, we rarely saw him after that. Scotland's a fair distance away. Just the odd visit.' A shadow of a smile, remembering.

I couldn't believe I was having this conversation. Calm, controlled, grown-up. I was pleased that I was able to carry it off – especially when I think of how much I had loathed the Arabella I had carried in my head all this time.

'So Mariella happened before I was born?' I realised she must be round about my own age but hadn't considered her date of birth.

'She was born on January 5th – you in March, so you're almost twins,' Arabella said, wiping her mouth on the paper napkin. 'But very different personalities – at least, that's what your dad used to say.'

Pasta finished, we studied the dessert menu. I hesitated. 'Go on,' Arabella said. 'Tiramisu? lemon sorbet? Gives me a good excuse.' I was beginning to enjoy this a lot. I hadn't had a meal out in years. It was never one of Mum's things, even when she was well. Dad, of course, was usually too busy – or so he said.

'What about your own work?' Arabella said. 'Are you taking art GCSE? What's your favourite medium, paint, like your dad? Pastel? Pen and ink?'

It was a lot to take in. A professional artist interested in what I was doing. 'With one thing and another, I haven't been doing very much recently,' I said. 'But I'm happiest with a pencil in my hand. I love the way it can make lines and create movement on the page – that's really exciting. And it's the easiest to use – you can carry a pencil around all the time.'

'Do you keep a sketchbook?'

'Yes,' I said.

'You'll let me look at it sometime? Please.'

'I'd love to,' I said and found I meant it.

A long silence. Coffee. 'I kept my promise, you know, didn't get in touch with your dad for years.' Arabella was anxious to get everything off her chest. 'Mariella must have been getting on for four when I had the opportunity to show my work in the arts centre in town. It was advertised in the local papers, but somehow I didn't expect your dad to pick it up. Well, maybe I was hoping if I'm honest. Anyway, he turned up. And lit the blue touch paper – again!' She made a wry face.

'What happened?' I felt I had to push it. 'I'm sorry. I shouldn't ask, but he's –was – my dad…'

'Not much, really, in the big scheme of things, but your mother found out that we were seeing one another again, well, it was more than that, you know?'

'I can imagine.'

'She went mad – literally – threatened suicide. In fact, she had a go, took an overdose and ended up in hospital.'

A long-hidden memory. Mum away, but for how long I had no idea. 'Your mum's in hospital,' they told me as I was parcelled out between Nan, Dad and a kindly neighbour. I remember feeling very excited – mothers and hospitals meant only one thing – a new baby! I was doomed to disappointment. When Mum arrived home, not only was she babyless, but she had changed out of all recognition.

'Turned into a different person,' Charles said.

Exactly. Almost overnight the fluffy child-mother I had known became a stricter, more conservative model. Out went the dirndl skirts, the puff-sleeved blouses, in came the tweedy suits, the sensible shoes, the pinned-up hair. 'The dragon lady,' my friends called her.

It must have been around this time that Dad started sleeping in the spare bedroom – not every night at first, but it soon developed into how things were. 'Your father and I have come to an arrangement,' Mum told me later when I realised Millie's parents didn't live this way. I had no idea what she was talking about.

From then on, I don't remember her laughing much – if ever. Being the Doctor's Wife (you could almost see the capital letters) was a serious business. As was living itself.

We adapted, Dad and I, although we were both under

strict control. Painting and drawing were our little foibles, to be tolerated from time to time with a show of minor martyrdom. It's amazing what you come to accept as a child. It's just how life is.

Equally amazing that, under these circumstances, Dad managed to produce such an exciting body of work. Perhaps her negative attitude spurred him on. Didn't Picasso say something along these lines?

'So that was that,' Arabella said in a flat voice. 'She held the very real threat of killing herself over your father's head, and he couldn't – or wouldn't – take the risk. "One motherless child in a family is enough" he used to say.'

'You didn't find anyone else?' I couldn't believe I was asking these personal questions.

'Nobody that mattered. It was Charles or no one. We rarely met again – only on the occasional painting weekend,' Arabella said.

I remembered Dad going off on painting jaunts from time to time. He used to whistle under his breath as he assembled brushes and paints, clean rags and endlessly interesting jars and pots, riding Mum's barbed jabs along the lines of 'it's all right for some.'

Then, quite suddenly, these painting away days stopped. No explanation. I don't even remember Mum looking victorious.

Arabella was lost in thought as she stirred her sugarless coffee. 'I didn't see him again until Mariella took ill the year before last. I had to get in touch, tell him what was happening.

We were both worried out of our minds about her, so I came back here where your dad could supervise Mariella's progress. He called in to see her almost every day and I was so thankful that he was around to share the strain.'

I tried and failed to imagine Dad doing his Dad-thing at Arabella's place, then coming back to do it all over again at home. How had he managed to keep his two lives going? At least, it answered the mystery of the spate of late visits and silent telephone calls.

The lunchtime crowd had thinned out. Tables were being cleared. It was time to go. Arabella reached for my hand. 'I loved your dad, really loved him – you must believe me.' I did.

I could feel tears threatening. Arabella too, despite her confident public face, was beginning to unravel at the edges.

Then she rallied, paid at the desk and ushered me outside. 'We need to get a move on,' she said. 'You and I have a Charles White exhibition to organise.'

CHAPTER TWELVE

'Arabella tells me you're not sure about your dad?' Nan quizzes me from across the room.

We are waiting for the taxi to take us into town – to the private view, the Charles White Retrospective, no less – well, Arabella, Nan and I are. We clutch our invitations with *The Dancing Daughter* in full colour on the cover, *Untitled,* the Llyncelyn landscape on the back.

Mariella has decided to give it a miss.

'I can put you right about your dad once and for all,' Nan says. 'Take your sandals off.' There we are, Nan and I, dressed to the nines, wriggling our bare toes. 'You too, Mariella.'

With a bit of a struggle, Nan puts her left foot up on a chair and pushes apart her third and fourth toes. 'See,' she points out. 'A star. My mother, your great-grandma had one, Charles too.'

Mariella grudgingly kicks off her flip-flops. She peers between her toes. Another star.

'Now you, Lucy.'

I prise my toes apart. No star.

'Try the other foot.' No star.

'Are you sure?' Nan can't believe it. 'Never mind,' she says, sounding flustered. 'Sometimes it might skip a generation. Wait till you have a baby. The star will return. Take my word for it.'

And do you know? I don't care. I've already turned down Henry's suggestion about having a DNA test. I *know* I'm Lucy White, the doctor's daughter. I don't need to prove it any more.

We climb into the taxi. 'Sure you don't want to come?' I ask my half-sister before I close the door.

'No thanks,' Mariella says. 'It's not really my scene.'

*

The papers are having a field day. *TRAGEDY OF ARTIST GP,* they shout. We're VIP guests, on our way to see Dad's work on show in the most prestigious gallery in town. It's a long time since I've seen Nan so excited. She is fizzing like a bottle of pop.

Arabella looks wonderful, as sexy as anyone her age can be. She's in black silky trousers and top, long silver and moonstone earrings (Dad's gift, she tells me) with a coloured cape thing in burgundy, orange, pink and purple swinging from her shoulders. She's the only person I know who could carry it off. Dad would have been proud of her.

Into the square, up the steps, through a glass door where the owner greets us with air kisses, a swift prickly brush on each cheek. 'Lovely to see you,' he breathes. 'It's a fantastic collection.'

'Pleased?' he asks Arabella.

'Delighted,' she nods, eyes wide – sparkling with excitement or shining with unshed tears? I'm not sure.

It's a glamorous, but incredibly noisy event. Famous people have stepped out of the TV screen to jostle one another and be seen. They are so busy balancing glasses of champagne and chatting that they rarely spare a glance at the paintings. One or two, however, comment knowledgeably on Charles White's use of colour, and his unusual technique, and guess the hidden meaning behind each picture.

Earwigging like mad, I'm so proud of my dad that I feel I might split open at any minute. 'Look,' I nudge Nan. 'Another red spot! How many have sold now?' I wander around, surreptitiously counting the red spots. Arabella too, is meandering about in a daze. 'If only...' we whisper to one another.

I see her lingering in front of one particular painting. Majestic hills streaked with clouds, a solitary house, patches of pale sunlight, deep shade. I check the title in my brochure, number 35, *Home in the Hills*. She smiles over her shoulder at someone. A reflection in the glass? Dad? Trick of the light.

She whispers, 'Your dad and I spent one magic weekend in that cottage. Terrible weather, I remember, not that it mattered to either of us.'

I point out the red spot. 'Someone's bought it?'

'Yes,' Arabella says. 'Me. I bagged it before the exhibition even opened.'

Such a pity that Mariella has chosen to stay at home. 'Can't see what all the fuss is about. After all, these pictures stood gathering dust for years and it made no difference to anyone. Charles obviously got some satisfaction from painting them and that's what matters – not people making fatuous comments.'

'But they'll be appreciated.' I tried hard to make her understand what an honour it is that dad's talent is at last being celebrated.

'So?' Mariella had shrugged. 'To think I was the one who started all this off because I needed some money to buy Cornflakes and things.'

'You have no soul,' her mother had said, shaking her head at her philistine daughter. It's really strange. Mariella is more like my mum's child than her own. Like her, she has little time for Dad and his painting – or for Arabella and her love of sculpture.

'It was all they ever talked about,' she told me. 'Boring, boring, boring.'

I bet she won't be so bored when she finds out what Dad's paintings are worth, I think to myself. Charles White is hot property these days, mentioned not only in the *Western Times,* but in *The Guardian* arts pages as well.

'Are we rich, Nan?' I ask.

'Mercenary creature! I'm surprised at you, Lucy-girl!' But there's a smile in her voice. 'I expect there's enough to put you through art college – and a bit left over for both of you. Let's not count our chickens,' she says.

She is led away to be interviewed by a television journalist. 'Is it true, Mrs. White, that your son's work was rescued from a skip?' I hear him ask.

'It wasn't quite like that,' she says, beginning again the story she's been telling all week.

Arabella and I are about to have a last tour of the gallery, when Henry appears, peering through the glass door at the jostling crowd. He gazes round in his short-sighted way. I grab his arm. 'I was beginning to think that you weren't coming,' I say.

'Do you imagine I'd miss a bash like this?' The white walls are ablaze with colour, each picture lit from above by its own mini-floodlight.

'A bit different from how they looked in the attic,' he says.

I escort Henry round the gallery, stopping at last in front of the stunning miniature of my naked mother, the only portrait in the collection. *The Dancing Daughter* has a NOT FOR SALE sign beneath it.

'It's the jewel in the crown,' the gallery owner comments in passing.

'I feel a proprietary interest in it too,' Henry says. He squeezes my hand and keeps hold of it. Henry? He looks down at me with something like affection in his eyes.

'*The Dancing Daughter* is *my* picture. Finder's keepers!' I tell him.

'Sure,' he says, aiming a kiss at the top of my head.

Yes, Dad's present to me. The swinging silver fish on the dancing figure catches the light. At my throat, a silver chain and hanging from it, that very fish – for real.

About the author

I was born and educated in Scotland. I became a primary teacher, married, had two daughters and was so busy just keeping things going at home and at school, that there was little time to try my hand at writing. I divorced, became a lecturer in Craigie College of Education in Ayr and began writing poetry, enjoying making words work for me.

My next job was as head of a primary school near Bristol and it was there that I started to write for children. After all, it's hardly fair to ask children to write a poem if you're not prepared to put your own words and ideas on the line. And believe me, primary children are the sternest of critics!

When I remarried, I moved to Wales, left full-time teaching and started a new career as a freelance writer. I'm lucky to be able to combine my teaching experience and interest in artwork and display with my love of writing. I have a number of books in publication, mostly those intended for use by primary school teachers. My first and possibly most successful is Language in Colour, published by Belair Publications Ltd. although my personal favourite is Paint a Poem, also from Belair.

After my lovely husband Allen died in 2003, I moved to Cornwall where I lived for ten years with my cat Bonnie. Although I visited fewer schools, I worked in the schoolroom of the RCH Hospital (Treliske) in Truro where the pupils were patients. This was an exciting and thoroughly worthwhile project – one that I now miss.

In 2005 I joined the prestigious Falmouth Poetry Group. The standard of my poetry came on by leaps and bounds and I made many friends among the members. I also set up the Cornish Chapter of the Society of Authors. I had two poetry collections published during my time in Cornwall, This Year, Next Year, and Firebird (IDP).

In 2013 I moved to Nunney, a village near Frome to live with Norman, a teaching colleague from the 80s – before I met Allen! We spend part of the year in Norman's house in Cyprus, enjoy jazz, (Norman has his own band: The New Academic Feetwarmers. I'm now a member of the Frome Writers' Collective and I've set up a new poetry-writing group. Of course, I continue to write! Poets don't give up easily! My current publishers are Poetry Space, Wish a Wish, Indigo Dreams Publishing and Publish & Print.

In 2021 along with Cornish poet Angie Butler, who has performed and had her work broadcast in the UK and Kenya, I co-authored my 101st book, Moonfall. It was Angie's first book.

Currently, I have several new illustrated children's stories being published by an American publisher – Sizemore.

Just a small selection of Moira's work:

123 books so far, and 2,500 poems in her archive!

Taste of Summer, Olympia 2025
Is She the Doctor's Daughter?, Publish and Print 2025
Thumbprints, Publish and Print 2022
Moonfall (with Angie Butler), Publish and Print 2021
Looking Through Water, Poetry Space 2020
Talking Book for the Blind, RNIB 2021
Poet in the Kitchen (with Jenny Ranson), Poetry Space 2020
Imagine a Kiss, Dempsey and Windle 2020
A Scream of many Colours, Poetry Space 2019
Geese and Daughters, Indigo Dreams 2018
Breakfast with Swallows, Austin Macauley 2017
A Box of Sky, Integral 2017 (English and Romanian translation)
Grandad's Party, Poetry Space 2016
Man in the Moon, Indigo Dreams 2014
Through a Child's Eyes, Poetry Space 2013
Wish a Wish, Poetry Space 2012
Firebird, Indigo Dreams 2011
The Dream Thing, Palores 2010
This Year, Next Year, 2004 (2nd edition 2008 Author House)
Fresh out of Dragonflies, Headlock 1995
Light the Blue Touch Paper, Iron Press 1986

Books for Teachers: Language and Colour, Words with Wings, Rainbow Year, Paint a Poem, Legend into Language, Patchwork of Poems, and Tell me a Tale (Belair Publications 1989 – 2002)

plus 18 children's illustrated storybooks, Sizemore 2021 -2025

Published by
www.publishandprint.co.uk

Printed in Great Britain
by Amazon